THE
PRIESTHOOD
IS
CHANGING

THE PRIESTHOOD IS CHANGING

By Kelley Varner

Destiny Image Publishers
P.O. Box 351
Shippensburg, PA 17257-0351

"We Publish the Prophets"

ISBN 1-56043-033-8

For Worldwide Distribution
Printed in the U.S.A.

First Printing: 1991
Second Printing: 1991

About The Cover

The cover depicts a side view of the Tabernacle of Moses as seen from the north. The wall has been removed that we might see Aaron the High Priest moving away from the Holy Place, toward the Most Holy Place. His back reveals the worn-out garments of the Levitical order of priesthood. His front shows the simplicity of the pure linen garments worn on the Feast Day of Atonement, the tenth day of the seventh month. He enters in glory, walking toward the Ark of God.

Acknowledgments

To Bill Edwards, whose practical instruction removed the intimidation of using my new computer.

To my wife Joann, who shared me with this manuscript for six weeks.

To the Holy Ghost, who is my Teacher.

Dedication

This book is not just a theological treatise; it is a manual for living. I dedicate it to two couples who are faithful priests, who have walked with God and with me for many years, and who are presently serving as elders with me at Praise Tabernacle. I give honor to whom honor is due.

Nat and Carolyn Rand, Charlie and Sue Baird, thank you for all that you have taught me, for helping me to understand people and the priesthood that we share.

Table of Contents

Foreword

Anne and I became acquainted with the ministry of Kelley Varner through audio tapes and numerous books. We invited him to minister at Rock Church, Virginia Beach, Virginia, in 1989. That was to be the first of many visits. We consider Kelley Varner an able minister of the New Testament, as well as a good friend.

During the latter part of the 80s, the world witnessed an unprecedented attack against the Body of Christ. Looking back, we now realize it was a calculated, diabolical plan aimed at destroying the credibility of the Church. What the enemy meant for evil, God meant for good, and judgment began in the house of the Lord. The Church has survived a bruising wound and, through the power of God, is well able to crush the head of the serpent.

It's time for all "true worshipers" to scripturally position themselves. God is no longer winking at spiritual ignorance and religious traditions, but is calling for the maturity of His saints.

The Priesthood Is Changing speaks of better things to come. It speaks of credibility and sincerity, maturity and holiness. The Body of Christ is listening for a mature sound. Many speak of it. But few can adequately describe it. However, when the believer hears it, he recognizes it.

Kelley Varner brings this "certain sound" in *The Priesthood Is Changing.*

The Reverends John and Anne Gimenez

Preface

Something has happened in the realm of the Spirit. It started at the beginning of this year, the beginning of this decade. God turned the corner. He has something up His sleeve...His arm. He is about to bare it in the eyes of every nation. All flesh shall see it together.

Everyone senses it. Like Samuel of old, the Holy Ghost has come to Bethlehem again. His mission is to anoint an exalted son in the midst of the brethren in the house of the Father. The prophet comes not with a vial, as he did in the time of Saul. No manmade vessel is sufficient for the things of this new day. Samuel has entered the city with a ram's horn, a Jubilee horn made by God, full of oil destined to be poured upon the chosen of the Lord.

Your inner man detects it. The hidden man of the heart is stirring in fresh expectation. He must have revival. Too long has he been frustrated with and bored by the sweat of Adam rather than the savor of Christ. The awareness of the fragrance of Him who called us now mingles with the atmosphere of His presence, determined to finish what He began.

Deep is calling to deep. Nothing matters now but the voice of our Beloved as He summons us from within the veil. This is the sound of life from the Mercy-seat. Some only hear thunder (John 12:29). Others are enamored by the messengers through whom He speaks. But this Voice now beckons us to leave the comforts and confines of our limitations, that we might walk on the water of His Word.

I did not plan to write this book. Frankly, I have not sensed this kind of intense inspiration for over three years. I recently sat in my living room imparting to a young pastor the essential differences between the Feast of Pentecost and the Feast of Tabernacles, between the Holy Place and the Most Holy Place. After laying the foundation for the third dimension in his spirit, I began to explain the parameters and the practical implications of this change of priesthood, especially in the areas of three relationships: the individual with the Lord, with the home and family and with the local church. I continued by clarifying the dynamics of this transition: why it was happening, how it would impact him and his local church, and how he could most wisely deal with its new effects. Lastly, I gave him the keys that Jesus is now speaking to apostolic and prophetic ministries to bring a new generation out of the wilderness and into the land.

As I heard these practical principles coming out of my mouth, the same ones I had spoken to dozens of other brothers in the past two years, the Spirit whispered, "Write the vision." Like the bush of old, the fire of God is burning in me, yet I am not consumed. You have turned aside to see; perchance you are among the ones He now dispatches to deliver His people. In the realm of gifts, one is concerned primarily with his own function and purpose. But in the realm of ministries, one is mostly concerned about the preparation of others to minister. If your heart is to equip the saints, read on.

I Sam. 2:35, KJV:

> *And I will raise me up a faithful priest, that shall do according to that which is in mine heart and in my mind: and I will build him a sure house; and he shall walk before mine anointed for ever.*

FAT AND LAZY

There is an existing Eli and a growing Samuel. A priesthood that is heavy of flesh is giving way to the administration of the Spirit. A ministry that is going blind and that refuses to restrain its sons is being replaced by the answered prayers of a woman in travail. An imitation man child named Ichabod has provoked us to prayer, and this intercession will give rise to a prophetic voice that will bring Israel back to God. This one is a faithful priest like David, Zadok, and the Lord Jesus Himself.

David was a faithful priest, a man after God's own heart. His mentor was an angry man, insane with jealousy and insecurity. Saul threw spears at people, even his own son Jonathan. So God changed the priesthood. He took the kingdom from Saul and gave it to David, dealing with the sweet psalmist for many years in many ways. This procedure was necessary...the Saul that was in David had to die. We don't need another madman on the throne.

Zadok was also a faithful priest, a key figure in David's cabinet. The name *Zadok* means "righteous," and is a nickname for *Melchisedec*, "king of righteousness." The story of Zadok and Abiathar, the story of two priesthoods, is too long to tell here. Abiathar appeared to be the natural successor as high priest; after all, he was of the tribe of Levi, his descent being traced back to Phineas, son of Eli. At this time in Bible history, there began to be less emphasis upon natural animal sacrifices as the main expression of worship, especially in connection with the Tabernacle of David. David used Zadok to set up a new order of worship with an emphasis upon singers, musicians, and praisers — spiritual sacrifices. Scribes from the ranks of the Levites began to record the songs of Zion. Unlike Abiathar's Levitical backdrop that emphasized outward obedience, David and Zadok ushered in an inward sense of the importance of righteousness that emphasized the condition of the heart. Later, in the Adonijah rebellion, Abiathar supported Adonijah while Zadok remained loyal to David and Solomon (First Kings 1).

The Bible is full of examples showing that the priesthood is changing. Above all, it is the spirit of this priesthood that is keying this change. Understand the difference between preaching and teaching and ministry: Ministry is the outflowing of the indwelling Christ, flowing from the heart and not the intellect. This new thing will be caught, not taught; it must be imparted. Men like Ezekiel are breathing a proceeding Word upon the bones of His Body. The Son is here. He is speaking. Let us have ears to hear all that He is about to say.

Chapter One

A Review of Threefold Things

Beyond Pentecost

In my book, *Prevail, A Handbook for the Overcomer*, 40 examples are given of the key principle for unlocking one's understanding of the Scripture: God's purpose is revealed in three dimensions.

Prov. 22:20-21, KJV:

> *Have not I written to thee excellent things in counsels and knowledge,*
>
> *That I might make thee know the certainty of the words of truth; that thou mightest answer the words of truth to them that send unto thee?*

"Excellent" things are literally "threefold" things. This truth is also detailed in the first chapter of *The More Excellent Ministry*, the sequel to *Prevail*. Everything is revealed in threes. Man, like God, is spirit, has a soul, and expresses himself through a body. When God gave the pattern (Ex. 25:40) of the Tabernacle to Moses in the wilderness, He revealed the Outer Court, the Holy Place, and the Most Holy Place. Reduced to one thought, I wrote in *Prevail* that there is something more in God beyond the realm of Pentecost, the Holy Place. *The More Excellent Ministry* introduced that "something more," telling of a Man in the throne with a ministry, and began to unveil the dynamics of His priesthood flowing from the throne of grace. This present volume, the third in the trilogy, lays out the nuts and bolts of the change from the old to the new. The three major feasts of the Lord, Passover, Pentecost, and Tabernacles, overlay the three dimensions of the Tabernacle of Moses, paralleling that pattern and scheme. The threshhold of this decade is the threshhold of a third feast, the threshhold of the Most Holy Place.

Deut. 16:16, KJV:

> *Three times in a year shall all thy males appear before the Lord thy God in the place which he shall choose; in the feast of unleavened bread, and in the feast of weeks, and in the feast of tabernacles: and they shall not appear before the Lord empty...*

David was anointed three times. The Pattern Son Jesus is presented as the Babe in the manger, the Youth in the Temple, and the Man in the Jordan (John 3:34). John in his epistle writes to little children, young men, and fathers (I John 2:12-14). In the Book of Numbers we read of workers, warriors, and worshipers. What does all this mean? It is best understood and communicated in terms of our Christian experience and our walk with the Lord.

The Feast of Passover

Our first meeting with Jesus took place in the Outer Court. We knelt at the foot of His cross, typified by the brazen altar. There we received forgiveness of sins through His blood (Eph. 1:6-7). The Holy Spirit convinced us of our nature as sinners and our need of a Savior. The Passover Lamb was slain for us and we experienced our beginnings in God.

Ex. 12:2, KJV:

This month shall be unto you the beginning of months: it shall be the first month of the year to you.

Ex. 12:13, KJV:

And the blood shall be to you for a token upon the houses where ye are: and when I see the blood, I will pass over you, and the plague shall not be upon you to destroy you, when I smite the land of Egypt.

1 Cor. 5:7-8, NIV:

Get rid of the old yeast that you may be a new batch without yeast—as you really are. For Christ, our Passover lamb, has been sacrificed.

Therefore let us keep the Festival, not with the old yeast, the yeast of malice and wickedness, but with bread without yeast, the bread of sincerity and truth.

1 Pet. 1:18-19, NIV:

For you know that it was not with perishable things such as silver or gold that you were redeemed from the empty way of life handed down to you from your forefathers, but with the precious blood of Christ, a lamb without blemish or defect.

We then sealed our conversion with water baptism in the Name of the Lord Jesus Christ for the remission of our sins and the circumcision of our heart (Acts 2:38; Col. 2:11-12; I John 5:8). He that believes and is baptized shall be saved (Mark 16:16). In Moses' Tabernacle, this took place at the brazen laver, a basin filled with water used for washing. An Outer Court Christian has been born again and baptized in water. But there is more. The new birth is but the beginning of our salvation. The Greek word for "salvation" is *soteria,* which describes a complete deliverance. God has determined to save the whole man: spirit, soul, and body.

I Thess. 5:23, KJV:

And the very God of peace sanctify you wholly; and I pray God your whole spirit and soul and body be preserved blameless unto the coming of our Lord Jesus Christ.

II Cor. 1:10, KJV:

...Who delivered us from so great a death, and doth deliver: in whom we trust that he will yet deliver us...

We have been saved. Our spirits have been saved and have passed from death to life. We have been translated (transferred) out of the kingdom of darkness into the Kingdom of God (Col. 1:9-13). That happened in the Outer Court. But we are also in the process of being saved. Our souls are being saved and transformed by the renovating of our minds. We have and are continuing to experience this exchange of minds, ours for His, in the Holy Place. Ultimately, we shall be saved. Our bodies shall be saved. We shall not all sleep. There is a generation who will put the last enemy under their feet. The glorious Church will realize that triumph in the Most Holy Place.

The Feast of Pentecost

Acts 2:4, NIV:

All of them were filled with the Holy Spirit and began to speak in other tongues as the Spirit enabled them.

Eph. 1:13-14, NIV:

And you also were included in Christ when you heard the word of truth, the gospel of your salvation. Having believed, you were marked in him with a seal, the promised Holy Spirit,

who is a deposit guaranteeing our inheritance until the redemption of those who are God's possession—to the praise of his glory.

Acts 19:1-2, NIV:

While Apollos was at Corinth, Paul took the road through the interior and arrived at Ephesus. There he found some disciples

and asked them, "Did you receive the Holy Spirit when you believed?" They answered, "No, we have not even heard that there is a Holy Spirit."

As the Feast of Pentecost was separate from and subsequent to the Feast of Passover, so is the pentecostal experience to regeneration. I was born again in the spring of 1966 and filled with the Holy Ghost two years later. Like the men of Ephesus, I had not heard of such things. I met Jesus the Baptizer at the Golden Candlestick in Moses' Tabernacle. There in that second room, the bowls of the Lampstand were filled with oil, one of the symbols of the Holy Spirit.

From 1968 to 1979, my Teacher and Guide opened my eyes, illuminating my spirit to see His Word, His Light (John 16:13). Then He showed me the piece of furniture adjacent to the Candlestick, the golden Table of Shewbread. As my walk with the Spirit progressed, I learned the meaning of covenant. As I continued to fellowship the mystery (Eph. 3:1-7), I saw that the border of the Table was a handbreadth and learned about the hand of God, the five ascension gift ministries of Ephesians 4:11. Then my Teacher took me to the third and final piece of furniture in the Holy Place, the Golden Altar, or the Altar of Incense. There He taught me how to pray in the Holy Ghost. The song of the Lord began to flow out of my heart as I learned to sing in and with the Spirit.

The Feast of Tabernacles

The Holy Ghost baptism was the key of David (Rev. 3:7) to me, unlocking the inexhaustible resources of the Feast of Pentecost. The Lord had filled me with the Spirit and then commanded me to be constantly filled (Eph. 5:18). How can a man be full of the Spirit and yet be hungry for more? God was about to enlarge my heart and increase my capacity for Him. He was about to unveil another room, a third room called "maturity," the King's chambers. In the early spring of 1979, I saw the Lord high and lifted up. I saw the Mercy-seat and the One seated between the cherubim. I saw that the purpose of Pentecost was consummated in the Most Holy Place.

Eph. 4:13, NIV:

...until we all reach unity in the faith and in the knowledge of the Son of God and become mature, attaining to the whole measure of the fullness of Christ.

Rom. 8:28-31, NIV:

And we know that all things work together for good to them that love God, to them who are the called according to his purpose.

For whom he did foreknow, he also did predestinate to be conformed to the image of his Son, that he might be the firstborn among many brethren.

Moreover whom he did predestinate, them he also called: and whom he called, them he also justified: and whom he justified, them he also glorified.

What shall we then say to these things? If God be for us, who can be against us?

1 John 3:1-2, NIV:

How great is the love the Father has lavished on us, that we should be called children of God! And that is what we are! The reason the world does not know us is that it did not know him.

> *Dear friends, now we are children of God, and what we will be has not yet been made known. But we know that when he appears, we shall be like him, for we shall see him as he is. Everyone who has this hope in him glorifies himself, just as he is pure.*

1 John 4:17, NIV:

> *Love is made complete among us so that we will have confidence on the day of judgment, because in this world we are like him.*

Once more, excellent things are threefold things. God's purpose is unfolding from within His people in three dimensions: the Outer Court, the Holy Place, and the Most Holy Place; the Feast of Passover, the Feast of Pentecost, and the Feast of Tabernacles.

The priesthood is changing. A new generation is crossing the river into the land. The rending of the Jordan in the days of Joshua pointed to the rending of the veil in the days of Jesus. Our Captain has cut off every hindrance from Adam's time forth (Josh. 3:16). As we follow the Ark, the Lordship of Jesus upheld by an ongoing priesthood, we must admit that we have not passed this way heretofore.

We are passing over.

Chapter Two

It Is Time to Draw Near

A New and Living Way

The epistle to the Hebrews is present truth to the Church of the 90s. The reason the author of this letter is anonymous is that our total focus might be upon the One who is the Word, the Lord Jesus Christ. Hebrews centers upon Him who was appointed Heir of all things (Heb. 1:1-3). The prophets and all they have spoken has been summed up in Jesus the Prophet. He is the brightness, the express image and character of the Father, upholding all things by the word of His power. His is a more excellent Name and ministry (Heb. 1:4; 8:6). It is to Him that we are being drawn (John 12:32). In a day when God is delivering His people from following personalities, Jesus is the Focus. Jesus is the Center. He is enthroned and exalted above all.

These are crucial days. Men everywhere are fainting. Pastors call weekly from across the nation, asking, "What is happening? What is going on?" The answer is obvious. The Day of the Lord is dawning and the Lord is revealing the hearts of men. The lid is coming off everything in the Day of the Lord.

I Cor. 3:13, KJV:

> *Every man's work shall be made manifest: for the day shall declare it, because it shall be revealed by fire; and the fire shall try every man's work of what sort it is.*

1 Cor. 3:13, NIV:

> *His work will be shown for what it is, because the Day will bring it to light. It will be revealed with fire, and the fire will test the quality of each man's work.*

Zeph. 1:12, NIV:

> *At that time I will search Jerusalem with lamps and punish those who are complacent, who are like wine left on its dregs, who think, "The Lord will do nothing, either good or bad."*

Zech. 2:1-2, KJV:

> *I lifted up mine eyes again, and looked, and behold a man with a measuring line in his hand.*
>
> *Then said I, Whither goest thou? And he said unto me, To measure Jerusalem, to see what is the breadth thereof, and what is the length thereof.*

The Heavenly Jerusalem, Zion, is the Church (Heb. 12:22-24). The Refiner now comes to measure the breadth and the length of His priesthood. How wide are we? What is the measure of our mercy and forgiveness, our commitment to others? How long are we? Who will we embrace and how far will we walk with them?

Isa. 33:13-14, KJV:

Hear, ye that are far off, what I have done; and, ye that are near, acknowledge my might.

The sinners in Zion are afraid; fearfulness hath surprised the hypocrites. Who among us shall dwell with the devouring fire? who among us shall dwell with everlasting burnings?

This fire is God Himself (Heb. 12:29), the Word in the mouth of His servants the prophets (John 1:1; Jer. 23:29). Draw near to the fire. As the ancient king discovered in the days of Daniel, God is in the furnace with His chosen. There is a formation taking place in the flames.

Who Are The Hebrews?

These are transitional days. The very name "Hebrews" confirms this, for it is the Old Testament word *eber*. It is taken from the root word *aw-bar* (Strong's #567) and means "to cross over; transition." It is rendered in the English as "passed over, come over, overcome, on the other side, beyond, region beyond, beyond the world, a shoot." Other Hebrew word studies reveal that the name "Hebrews" carries the main idea of movement of one thing in relationship to another, the second object being stationary. The Greek concept is based upon the Hebrew meaning, which had four basic aspects:

1. *It meant "to go beyond or further."*
2. *It spoke of movement between two places.*
3. *It was used as a metaphor meaning "to exceed."*

4. It carried a moral or spiritual meaning of "to transgress."

As seen in the previous chapter, our growth in God is in three dimensions. The Church is at a crossroads. We have experienced our childhood and youth in God, having been born again and filled with the Spirit. Now it is time to go on, time to grow up in Him, time to enter the third dimension, the place of maturity. It is time to draw near as we pass over into another move of God.

Just as Jehovah brought the Old Testament "church" (Acts 7:38) out of Egypt, through the wilderness and into the land, so now He brings a new generation across Jordan to conquer Jericho. The manna has ceased. Bread from Heaven has sustained us for forty years, bringing us to this day. It kept us and laid the foundation for what God is saying and doing at this moment. Our portion today is the mature corn of the land. Our diet has changed. The writer to the Hebrews explains:

Heb. 5:12-6:3, NIV:

In fact, though by this time you ought to be teachers, you need someone to teach you the elementary truths of God's word all over again. You need milk, not solid food!

Anyone who lives on milk, being still an infant, is not acquainted with the teaching about righteousness.

But solid food is for the mature, who by constant use have trained themselves to distinguish good from evil.

Therefore let us leave the elementary teachings about Christ and go on to maturity, not laying again the foundation of repentance from acts that lead to death, and of faith in God,

instruction about baptisms, the laying on of hands, the resurrection of the dead, and eternal judgment.

And God permitting, we will do so.

Heaven won't issue a building permit until the foundation has passed the specifications of the building code. What worked yesterday will not work today. Moses is dead. The old order, like the law, has brought nothing to conclusion. This new generation must be circumcised, receive a heavenly strategy from the Captain of the host, and celebrate the Passover of conquest (Joshua 5).

At this point, every Christian must see that there are two kinds of people described in the epistle to the Hebrews:

1. *Those who draw near with full assurance of faith.*
2. *Those who draw back unto perdition.*

Heb. 10:19-22, NIV:

Therefore, brothers, since we have confidence to enter the Most Holy Place by the blood of Jesus,

by a new and living way opened for us through the curtain, that is, his body,

and since we have a great priest over the house of God,

let us draw near to God with a sincere heart in full assurance of faith, having our hearts sprinkled to cleanse us from a guilty conscience and having our bodies washed with pure water.

Heb. 10:38-39, NIV:

But my righteous one will live by faith. And if he shrinks back, I will not be pleased with him.

But we are not of those who shrink back and are destroyed, but of those who believe and are saved.

The historical background of this epistle reveals the same dilemma and conflict. Because of persecution, many of the Hebrew Christians were committing one of two evils: they were either going back altogether to Judaism, or they were trying to put new wine into old wineskins by mixing law with grace.

The extremes of the faith message have circumvented the cross, yet God's Word still calls us to the fellowship of His sufferings (Isa. 48:10). The Jacob nature within man is waiting for the price to be right. As tribulations and pressures increase, men are seeking more familiar surroundings. They ferret out old reference points, desperate for something to hold onto in the day of shaking. Others compromise and preach just enough present truth to be palatable without making the saints uncomfortable. These have sodden the Lamb and watered down the reality of our need to become a whole burnt offering. But there is a price to the prize. There is a high calling, and there is a people who will follow the Lamb at all costs (Phil. 3:12-14; Rev. 14:1-5).

Heb. 12:26-29, NIV:

At that time his voice shook the earth, but now he has promised, "Once more I will shake not only the earth but also the heavens."

The words "once more" indicate the removing of what can be shaken—that is, created things—so that what cannot be shaken may remain.

Therefore, since we are receiving a kingdom that cannot be shaken, let us be thankful, and so worship God acceptably with reverence and awe,

for our God is a consuming fire.

Three Relationships

This is not a day to draw back. It is a day to draw near. We are passing over in three basic relationships:

1. *The individual and his walk with the Lord.*
2. *The individual and his home and family.*
3. *The individual and his local church.*

First of all, it is time for each one of us to draw near to the Lord. Throughout the land, we hear a fresh emphasis on prayer and waiting before Him (Isa. 40:31). Secondly, there is a renewed vision for the restoration of our homes. Husbands and wives are heirs together of the grace of life. In a domestic sense, they are a mighty apostolic team sent to their children and neighbors (I Pet. 3:7). Thirdly, this is not a time to stay away from the house of the Lord. We are to be assembled together, literally and spiritually (Heb. 10:25). If you are drawing back from godly leadership that is hearing from the Lord, you are listening to the wrong voice.

Esther drew near. It was a matter of life and death. The first five chapters of her book tell of the providence of God bringing a Jewish maiden to the throne. Vashti refused to display her beauty and was disqualified from rulership. The king was desirous of one who would show forth his virtues and praise. After having been purified with things bitter and things sweet, Esther prepared to draw near to Ahasuerus. While the other girls adorned themselves with Babylonian trinkets, Esther obeyed the voice of the servant Hegai (a type of the Holy Ghost), for he knew what pleased the king. Later, because of the devilish decree of Haman, Queen Esther drew near once again. She put on her royal apparel and approached the throne. The king granted her favor and extended to her the golden scepter, the emblem of his authority and headship.

Esth. 5:1-2, KJV:

> *Now it came to pass on the third day, that Esther put on her royal apparel, and stood in the inner court of the king's house, over against the king's house: and the king sat upon his royal throne in the royal house, over against the gate of the house.*
>
> *And it was so, when the king saw Esther the queen standing in the court, that she obtained favour in his sight: and the king held out to Esther the golden sceptre that was in his hand. So Esther drew near, and touched the top of the sceptre.*

The word for "top" here means "captain, chiefest place, excellent, first, forefront, highest part" and speaks of the authority of the Head of the Church (Eph. 1:20-23). There is a people who are forsaking all to apprehend Him who is the Head over all. We are laying hold of Him who has "apprehended" us (Phil. 3:12-14). This word is *katalambano* and is taken from two Greek words:

1. *kata* = "down," and
2. *lambano* = "to seize, grasp, lay hold of."

God came down and embraced humanity through His Son. In the incarnation, Jesus descended to the level of men of low estate. This was the embrace of His own faith, His own conviction that He is able to complete His purposes in man. Now He longs for a people who will embrace Him with the same intensity with which He has embraced them (John 3:16).

The priesthood is changing. There's nothing to go back to. Our crutches, our familiar fleshly supports, our idols, are gone; our Father has graciously burned them with fire. It's a new day, a fresh beginning in Him, and now there is hope. Jesus is restoring our wineskins as He soaks us in the water of His Word and then rubs us with the oil of His Spirit. Without fear, we can now get up and learn to walk again.

Matt. 7:13-14, NIV:

Enter through the narrow gate. For wide is the gate and broad is the road that leads to destruction, and many enter through it.

But small is the gate and narrow the road that leads to life, and only a few find it.

Chapter Three

He Taketh Away the First

The Changing of the Covenants

We have reviewed threefold things. We have sensed the urgency to draw near, to press on to know the Lord. The Lord has ministered fresh hope to our spirits. Now His disciples must grasp another truth: God takes away the first that He might establish the second.

Heb. 10:9, KJV:

> *Then said he, Lo, I come to do thy will, O God. He taketh away the first, that he may establish the second.*

Heb. 10:9, NIV:

> *Then he said, "Here I am, I have come to do your will." He sets aside the first to establish the second.*

He took away the first covenant, the Old Testament, that He might establish the second covenant, the New Testament. In the context of Hebrews 10, He took away the first Body that He might establish the second Body. He took away the body of Jesus in ascension that He might establish the Church, the Body of Christ, through the power of the Comforter who was to come.

The Greek word for "taketh away" in Hebrews 10:9 means "to take away with violence." The word for "establish" in the same verse is *histemi* and means "to stand." Interestingly, the Greek word for "resurrection" is in the same word family as the latter; it is *anastasis*, taken from two words:

1. *ana* = "again," and
2. *histemi* = "to stand."

Strong's Concordance renders *anastasis* as "a standing up again." God took away the Old Covenant with violence, even the violence of the cross! He then established the New Covenant as Jesus Christ was declared to be the Son of God with power, according to the Spirit of holiness, by His resurrection from the dead (Rom. 1:4). His violent death and glorious resurrection are the basis of the New Testament in His blood.

Two Covenants

This present chapter is a pivotal one, essential to our understanding of the fact that the priesthood is changing. It is similar to Chapter Seven of *The More Excellent Ministry*, which reveals a ministry without idolatry. There we discovered that two images are two covenants, and noted that "the Bible is divided into two covenants, the Old Testament and the New Testament. While these parts have a historical setting and meaning, it is more important to realize that they embody spiritual principles. Thus the Old Testament speaks of the old nature, the

New Testament of the new nature" (p. 207; see also pp. 222-26).

In the same chapter we learned that the "natural face" of James 1:23 is our "genesis face" or "the face of our birth." Our "natural face" is the face of a new nature . . . the Man in the mirror is the new man! The glory of the Old Testament and the old nature was mirrored in the face of Moses; the glory of the New Testament and the new nature is now revealed in the face of Jesus Christ (II Cor. 3:17-4:6).

II Cor. 3:18, KJV:

> But we all, with open face beholding as in a glass the glory of the Lord, are changed into the same image from glory to glory, even as by the Spirit of the Lord.

From glory to glory; out of glory and into glory . . . out of the glory of the law and into the glory of grace and truth (John 1:17). Out of the glory of man and into the glory of the Lord, out of the passing and into the permanent (I Pet. 1:24). Jesus fulfilled the law and the prophets. He has consecrated for us a new and living way through His blood.

John 19:30, NIV:

> When he had received the drink, Jesus said, "It is finished." With that, he bowed his head and gave up his spirit.

Matt. 27:50-53, NIV:

> And when Jesus had cried out again in a loud voice, he gave up his spirit.

At that moment the curtain of the temple was torn in two from top to bottom. The earth shook and the rocks split.

The tombs broke open and the bodies of many holy people who had died were raised to life.

They came out of the tombs, and after Jesus' resurrection they went into the holy city and appeared to many people.

The veil was rent from the top to the bottom. The law was finished. Grace and truth had prevailed. An age, an order, an era, had changed. This happened 2,000 years ago . . . historically, literally. Our Savior died with violence to take away the first covenant, then rose in triumph to forever establish the New Covenant.

Know this: these same covenantal principles are operative every time God changes an order, whether it be national or personal. These are the active ingredients of every revival of Church history, every fresh outpouring of the Holy Ghost, especially the present one. These same truths apply to the progressive unfolding of the Christ nature in the life of the individual Christian.

The covenants changed. Look more closely and discover a change of order in many facets and applications. But whenever man locks himself inside a time-space world, he blinds himself to the unsearchable riches of Christ. God created time, so He is larger than time. Jesus is Truth and Jesus is God; therefore the components of truth concerning a changing priesthood are larger than time.

The order is changing . . . again. Don't misunderstand me. There won't be another covenant. One of the major weaknesses of traditional dispensationalism is its theory that the New Covenant is essentially Jewish and still to come, including the trappings of animal sacrifices. The New Covenant of Jeremiah 31 and Hebrews 8 is the New Testament, pure and simple. His was *the* Sacrifice, once and for all! (For the serious student, a verse-by-verse exegesis of those two chapters is available in my notes on the prophecy of Jeremiah.)

Read the Book of Hebrews again. Jesus is the last Word on the subject! There won't be another covenant, another priesthood, another anything. Jesus is better than Moses, and Aaron, and Joshua, and the angels. His promises, His priesthood, His blood, is better. Everything about Jesus in that epistle is "better," literally "nobler or stronger." Some have stopped holding the Head (Col. 2:19) and have contrived a "third covenant," but they have gone beyond that which is written to substantiate it (Rev. 22:18). Jesus is the Alpha and the Omega, the Beginning and the End. His death and resurrection changed the priesthood and the order of the testaments permanently. His king-priest ministry after the order (manner, similitude) of Melchisedec is immutable. But the principles of that change take place whenever God moves in a fresh way among men. From Martin Luther to the present, God has been restoring all things.

Bombs Away!

Isa. 28:9-10, KJV:

> *Whom shall he teach knowledge? and whom shall he make to understand doctrine? them that are weaned from the milk, and drawn from the breasts.*

For precept must be upon precept, precept upon precept; line upon line, line upon line; here a little, and there a little...

Joel 2:25, KJV:

And I will restore to you the years that the locust hath eaten, the cankerworm, and the caterpillar, and the palmerworm, my great army which I sent among you.

Acts 3:19-21, KJV:

Repent ye therefore, and be converted, that your sins may be blotted out, when the times of refreshing shall come from the presence of the Lord;

And he shall send Jesus Christ, which before was preached unto you:

Whom the heaven must receive until the times of restitution of all things, which God hath spoken by the mouth of all his holy prophets since the world began.

The purposes of God come in threes. When God moved from the Outer Court to the Holy Place, from the Feast of Passover to the Feast of Pentecost, the order changed . . . the priesthood changed. From the Reformation of the early 1500s to the outpouring at Azuza Street in 1906, men walked in the truths of justification by faith (Martin Luther), water baptism (the Anabaptists), sanctification (John Wesley), and divine healing (A. B. Simpson).

Then God dropped a bomb! Men such as Charles Parham and William Seymour were anointed to proclaim the second feast. Each of us who has been filled with the Holy Ghost can deeply appreciate our Pentecostal roots, our fathers and mothers in the Lord. Those pioneers hungered and thirsted after righteousness and were filled. They were mocked and scorned by those who were content with but the first feast. Those trailblazers were shot at and their churches burned. Persecution was the price they paid for truth. Their prayers and prophecies have birthed us and brought us to this day. We are grateful and proud to be called "Pentecostal."

At this point, we emphasize that the greater feast always swallows up and includes all the truth and glory of the previous feast. Pentecost includes Passover, and the current Feast of Tabernacles includes Passover and Pentecost. We cannot do away with the foundation, the underpinning, the first principles. Our passion is to finish the building and hasten the coming of Him who is the Capstone! To preach the "full Gospel" is to preach Jesus all the way from the Outer Court to the Most Holy Place. He is Savior, Baptizer, and King! In Psalm 22 Jesus is the Savior; in Psalm 23, the Shepherd; in Psalm 24, the Sovereign. He is Jesus, the Christ, my Lord. He is the Sum of all.

From 1900 to 1948, men explored the New Covenant realities of the Holy Place, the Feast of Pentecost. Then, on February 13, 1948, about a year and three months before I was born, God dropped another bomb! Richard Riss, in his wonderful documentary, *Latter Rain*, details those days of the late 40s and the early 50s. Men like George Hawtin, George Warnock, Bill Britton, and many others were anointed to proclaim yet another feast! These radical Christians were mocked and scorned by those who were content with but two feasts. Persecution was the price they paid for truth. Their prayers and prophecies have birthed us and brought us to this day. Sound familiar?

God has been restoring truth line upon line from the 1500s to the present. Historically, the Feast of Passover and the truths of the Outer Court began to be restored with Martin Luther. The Feast of Pentecost and the truths of the Holy Place began to be restored with men such as Parham and Seymour at Azuza Street. The Feast of Tabernacles and the truths of the Most Holy Place began to be restored over forty years ago! The blowing of the trumpets, which took place on the first day of the seventh month, began to blow before I exited my mother's womb.

On the Feast Day of Atonement, which takes place on the tenth day of the seventh month, God deals with sin. All of us collided with the recent season of Jesus' cleansing His Church, especially its leaders. This deep dealing will continue for at least the first three years of this decade. Then God will have Himself a many-membered sickle, a new sharp threshing instrument having teeth with which He will thresh the mountains (Isa. 41:15). The Lord of the harvest is beginning to garner, not just individuals, but families, cities and nations! There has begun an international explosion of evangelism as the Feast of Tabernacles is being fulfilled in and through the Church. Still we hear the adolescent rantings of those who desire to be on the "cutting edge" of what they suppose to be the current move of God. Most will have to run to catch up. This is why new wine cannot be put into an old wineskin. This is why this book became the burden of the Lord: to tell the brethren that a second-day agenda is obsolete in the third day.

Chapter Four

To the Jew First

History Repeats Itself

Did you understand the previous chapter? It is crucial and necessary that these principles bypass your intellect and lodge in your heart. This new feast is of the Spirit. The Kingdom is in the Holy Ghost (Rom. 14:17). He takes away the first that He might establish the second. Whenever God does that, He always comes to the Jew first.

Rom. 1:16, KJV:

> *For I am not ashamed of the gospel of Christ: for it is the power of God unto salvation to every one that believeth; to the Jew first, and also to the Greek.*

Matt. 10:5-6, KJV:

> *These twelve Jesus sent forth, and commanded them, saying, Go not into the way of the Gentiles, and into any city of the Samaritans enter ye not.*
>
> *But go rather to the lost sheep of the house of Israel.*

Acts 3:24-26, NIV:

"Indeed, all the prophets from Samuel on, as many as have spoken, have foretold these days.

And you are heirs of the prophets and of the covenant God made with your fathers. He said to Abraham, 'Through your offspring all peoples on earth will be blessed.'

When God raised up his servant, he sent him first to you to bless you by turning each of you from your wicked ways."

The priesthood is changing. The Church is moving from the Holy Place to the Most Holy Place, from the Feast of Pentecost to the Feast of Tabernacles, from adolescence to maturity. The above verses are not to be proof texts for traditional dispensationalism. These Scriptures show us what happened historically in the changing of the covenants. In the Gospels and the Book of Acts, Jesus offered the New Covenant to the Jew first. He came to the people and the generation who had been the recipients of the previous order, who had received His Word into their hearts.

John 1:11-13, KJV:

He came unto his own, and his own received him not.

But as many as received him, to them gave he power to become the sons of God, even to them that believe on his name:

Which were born, not of blood, nor of the will of the flesh, nor of the will of man, but of God.

We have already learned that the Old Testament's giving way to the New is not just a chronological and historical fact, a spiritual saga of the past. Within that transition are the working parts and the glory of each step of God's progressive handiwork and determination to restore His creation. These principles can be applied to our individual walk with the Lord or, in a much broader sense, to every move of God from Luther until today. Among them is the one we underline now: God always comes to the Jew first. He searches the earth for the people who were the witnesses and recipients of the preceding outpouring, the people to whom He had committed and entrusted the oracles of God.

Rom. 2:28-3:2, KJV:

For he is not a Jew, which is one outwardly; neither is that circumcision, which is outward in the flesh:

But he is a Jew, which is one inwardly; and circumcision is that of the heart, in the spirit, and not in the letter; whose praise is not of men, but of God.

What advantage then hath the Jew? or what profit is there of circumcision?

Much every way: chiefly, because that unto them were committed the oracles of God.

Rom. 2:28-3:2, NIV:

A man is not a Jew if he is only one outwardly, nor is circumcision merely outward and physical.

No, a man is a Jew if he is one inwardly; and circumcision is circumcision of the heart, by the Spirit, not by the written code. Such a man's praise is not from men, but from God.

What advantage, then, is there in being a Jew, or what value is there in circumcision?

Much in every way! First of all, they have been entrusted with the very words of God.

John 1:1, KJV:

In the beginning was the Word, and the Word was with God, and the Word was God.

John 1:14, KJV:

And the Word was made flesh, and dwelt among us, (and we beheld his glory, the glory as of the only begotten of the Father,) full of grace and truth.

John 3:16, KJV:

For God so loved the world, that he gave his only begotten Son, that whosoever believeth in him should not perish, but have everlasting life.

A real Jew has had a circumcision of heart. When God gets ready to move in the earth, He frisks the Body for those who had received the Word in the previous move, especially those whose heart had been open, those who had loved His Word. A true Jew has heard the Word in his heart.

The most precious Gift of all is the Word of God. When the time came for God to bless the earth with the unspeakable Gift (II Cor. 9:15), He sent the Word, He sent Himself. The word for "oracles" in Romans 3:2 is *logion* (Strong's #3051), which means "an utterance of God." It is used four times: the verse above, Acts 7:38, Hebrews 5:12, and First Peter 4:11. It is a derivative of *logos* (#3056), translated "the Word" in John 1:1, 14 and taken in turn from the root word *lego* (#3004), "to lay forth, to relate in words, usually of systematic or set discourse."

Everything God wanted to say to man is in Jesus, the Word. When He came forth from the bosom of the Father, there was an army of words in His loins. Unlike other words which are used to speak of an individual expression, *lego* refers to a related group or family of words and is prophetically indicating a group of words, a team of words that minister together, a company of ordered words, the host of the heavenlies . . . the many-membered Body of Christ in union with its Head, Jesus, the Word of God! Each of us is a word and, tied together in relationships, we form a sentence, then a paragraph, then a page, then a chapter, and ultimately a book . . . the volume of the Book . . . the Lamb's Book of Life. The opening of that Book is the manifestation of the sons of God, the unveiling of the Son within His Church, God's epistle (II Cor. 3:1-2). That Book will judge the world (I Cor. 6:1-4). That Book, that Body, is the Church.

God Always Comes to His Own

When the cloud was ready to move from the Outer Court to the Holy Place, from the Feast of Passover to the Feast of Pentecost, the Holy Ghost began to offer the second feast to those who had known and experienced Jesus the Savior, the Sanctifier and the Healer. God went to the people to whom He had entrusted His Word. He went to those among the evangelicals and the holiness movements who had heard the Word in their hearts. This happened at the turn of the century and is well documented by the histories of all the major Pentecostal denominations as well as independent writings. It is a fascinating and wonderful story, an energized memory giving way to a liberated tongue, producing a radical hope to bring forth a passionate dream. The roots of every Spirit-filled Christian on the planet can be traced to a little mission on Azuza Street. How sad that in 1906 many "Jews" refused to acknowledge anything beyond the first feast.

Luke 19:41-44, NIV:

As he approached Jerusalem and saw the city, he wept over it

and said, "If you, even you, had only known on this day what would bring you peace—but now it is hidden from your eyes.

The days will come upon you when your enemies will build an embankment against you and encircle you and hem you in on every side.

They will dash you to the ground, you and the children within your walls. They will not leave one stone on another, because you did not recognize the time of God's coming to you."

Luke 19:44, KJV:

And shall lay thee even with the ground, and thy children within thee; and they shall not leave in thee one stone upon another; because thou knewest not the time of thy visitation.

A person, a family, a local church, a city, a nation . . . can miss the day of His visitation.

The Lord Jesus always comes to His own. When He was about to announce that there was more than the Feast of Pentecost, He again went to the Jew first. In the late 1940s and the early 1950s, Jesus spoke to those who had known and experienced Him as the One who baptizes with the Holy Ghost, to those with the truths of Pentecost in their hearts. How sad that in 1948 many "Jews," the sons and daughters, the grandsons and granddaughters of the pioneers of Pentecost, failed to acknowledge or discern anything beyond the first two feasts.

Trumpets began to blow over 40 years ago. God was moving on. A clear word heralded the journeying of the camp, calling the holy nation to a new dimension of spiritual warfare in the heavenlies; it announced the Feast of Tabernacles. In the 1950s the ministry of the evangelist demonstrated to the world what God could do in the supernatural display of signs, wonders and miracles. In the 1960s He poured out His Spirit upon the denominations and raised up anointed teachers to help His people. In the 1970s this army of raw recruits needed to know the reality of spiritual authority and discipline, so God brought forth pastors and shepherds to feed His sheep. The 1980s saw the resurgence of the ministry of the prophet, and the 1990s will be marked by the restoration of apostles, the ministry of the fathers.

From 1948 to the present, Jesus' intention has been to bring His Church into the Holiest of All. Especially since 1979, when He revealed to apostles and prophets that the

Most Holy Place is a present reality, the Lord has been relentless in pursuing a people for His Name. We are the sons and the daughters, the grandsons and the granddaughters, of a generation that was brought to Kadesh-Barnea (Num. 13-14) and who provoked the Lord by their unbelief. That generation was content to raid the heavenly places (Eph. 1:3) but twice a year, in the spring and in the fall. Now the Lord is inviting His people to live in the land of milk and honey. Wake up, Church! We don't have to wander in the wilderness for another 40 years.

Heb. 3:17-4:2, NIV:

> *And with whom was he angry for forty years? Was it not with those who sinned, whose bodies fell in the desert?*

> *And to whom did God swear that they would never enter his rest if not to those who disobeyed ?*

> *So we see that they were not able to enter, because of their unbelief.*

> *Therefore, since the promise of entering his rest still stands, let us be careful that none of you be found to have fallen short of it.*

> *For we also have had the gospel preached to us, just as they did; but the message they heard was of no value to them, because those who heard did not combine it with faith.*

Heb. 4:1-2, KJV:

> *Let us therefore fear, lest, a promise being left us of entering into his rest, any of you should seem to come short of it.*

For unto us was the gospel preached, as well as unto them: but the word preached did not profit them, not being mixed with faith in them that heard it.

The Joshua Generation

Out of every camp and every stream is coming a Most Holy Place people, the glorious Church. Out of every denomination and nondenominational denomination now walks forth a people to experience and enjoy the Feast of Tabernacles. From every tribe is coming His Tribe, from every race and nation His Holy Nation. Our first love is not to preach a message, but to come into union with a Person, that we might release His life to others.

I Pet. 2:9-10, KJV:

But ye are a chosen generation, a royal priesthood, an holy nation, a peculiar people; that ye should shew forth the praises of him who hath called you out of darkness into his marvellous light:

Which in time past were not a people, but are now the people of God: which had not obtained mercy, but now have obtained mercy.

This generation is mixing the Word with faith. This Joshua generation is possessing the land and causing others to inherit. Dangerously filled with the Holy Ghost, this army of the Lord is taking the battle to the gate. We are facing satan on his own turf, for we are fearless, aggressive and bold as lions.

In the historical Feast of Tabernacles, the people of God left the comfort of their homes and lived in booths.

They took to the streets. The Feast of Tabernacles will be a street revival. All men shall hear the good news, and every segment, section and strata of society will be invaded with the Gospel of the Kingdom (Matt. 24:14).

God has sovereignly opened the ears of men to hear the Word of the Lord. Each day, more and more people become hungry to hear present truth. Five years ago these same folks would bolt and run from hearing anything more than Pentecost. Now they are being strategically placed by the Holy Ghost for the coming revival.

Prov. 20:12, KJV:

The hearing ear, and the seeing eye, the Lord hath made even both of them.

Prov. 20:12, NIV:

Ears that hear and eyes that see—the Lord has made them both.

The greatest blessing in your life is that you can still hear. Your hunger and thirst for things permanent, not things passing, is your only hope for the days ahead. To you has been committed the most precious Gift of all . . . His Word. God is speaking. He is coming to the Jew first. See that you refuse not Him that speaks.

Chapter Five

An Overview of the Change

Nine Major Principles

In Chapter One we discovered that there is a third feast, another feast beyond Pentecost. Chapter Two encouraged us to draw near to the holiest of all. In Chapter Three we learned that the changing of the priesthood involved the changing of the covenants. In the previous chapter we uncovered another principle: When God transforms the order or begins a new phase in our lives, He always comes to the Jew first. Now that we have been introduced to these basic themes, we are ready to look at several major differences between the Holy Place and the Most Holy Place, between the Feast of Pentecost and the Feast of Tabernacles, between spiritual adolescence and spiritual maturity.

The remainder of this treatise will examine the following contrasts, sampling the pragmatics, the nuts and bolts of a changing priesthood. In each of these examples, the primary thought underlying the Principle of the Holy Place is that of mixture, while the dominant theme of the Most Holy Place is union with Christ. Keep in mind that each point also contrasts the Old Testament and the New Testament. A change of priesthood is a change of covenants. We will study these nine primary issues:

1. **The future and the present.**
2. **Duality and simplicity.**
3. **Two wills and one will.**
4. **The prophets and the Prophet.**
5. **Mount Sinai and Mount Zion.**
6. **Healing and the Healer.**
7. **Seeking God's hand and seeking God's face.**
8. **Taking tithes and receiving tithes.**
9. **Man's control and God's control.**

II Pet. 1:12, KJV:

> *Wherefore I will not be negligent to put you always in remembrance of these things, though ye know them, and be established in the present truth.*

These principles of present truth are meat and drink for the inner man, the hidden man of the heart, the real you, the man of the spirit. Presented in the practical context of the home and the local church, they point out our present position in the purposes of God, what to expect as He changes the priesthood, and how to deal with ourselves and others in this new day. The administration of the Spirit is changing, and it is especially important that pastors and elders understand how the Chief Shepherd is currently dealing with His people. These spiritual trends are summed up in the following principles:

1. The Melchisedec Principle.
2. The Measure Principle.
3. The Marriage Principle.
4. The Mouthpiece Principle.
5. The Mountain Principle.
6. The Man Principle.
7. The Motive Principle.
8. The Money Principle.
9. The Management Principle.

God has already begun to open your heart concerning these areas of truth. I have asked Him to grace me with words which the Holy Ghost teaches, words which you can clearly understand (I Cor. 2:9-14). Some of this is going to sound new, but as you listen for His voice in your spirit, you will experience an ongoing awareness of who you already are in Christ. I am not your teacher, He is. Be like the Bereans, maintaining an open heart and ear. Come now into the banqueting house. The table is filled with things new and old. Eat as much as you want. I am grateful and honored to serve you.

Acts 17:10-11, NIV:

As soon as it was night, the brothers sent Paul and Silas away to Berea. On arriving there, they went to the Jewish synagogue.

Now the Bereans were of more noble character than the Thessalonians, for they received the message with great eagerness and examined the Scriptures every day to see if what Paul said was true.

Acts 17:11, KJV:

These were more noble than those in Thessalonica, in that they received the word with all readiness of mind, and searched the scriptures daily, whether those things were so.

Matt. 13:52, KJV:

Then said he unto them, Therefore every scribe which is instructed unto the kingdom of heaven is like unto a man that is an householder, which bringeth forth out of his treasure things new and old.

Chapter Six

The Melchisedec Principle

Two Thieves: The Past and the Future

Spread before our eyes are nine plateaus of His promised land. As we begin our journey, remember that these nine principles overlap and interrelate; they are applicable in a number of ways. Whether the topic at hand concerns the changes and growth patterns of the individual believer or the shifts now taking place in movements or nations, these truths will guide us to our present place in the volume of the Book.

The priesthood is changing, moving from the perspective of the future to the perspective of the present, from man's point of view to God's point of view, for He sees the end from the beginning. This is called the "Melchisedec Principle" because His priesthood is ever present, now proceeding from the heart of our Ascended Lord.

Song 4:8, KJV:

Come with me from Lebanon, my spouse, with me from Lebanon: look from the top of Amana, from the top of Shenir and Hermon, from the lions' dens, from the mountains of the leopards.

Phil. 3:20, KJV:

For our conversation is in heaven; from whence also we look for the Saviour, the Lord Jesus Christ...

Num. 13:33, KJV:

And there we saw the giants, the sons of Anak, which come of the giants: and we were in our own sight as grasshoppers, and so we were in their sight.

Num. 14:9, KJV:

Only rebel not ye against the Lord, neither fear ye the people of the land; for they are bread for us: their defence is departed from them, and the Lord is with us: fear them not.

Jesus Christ, our heavenly Bridegroom, invites His Bride to view the land from the top of the mountain. Having been transferred from the kingdom of darkness to the Kingdom of Light, we now sit together with Him in heavenly places (Eph. 2:1-6). From the heights of His vantage point, the place of adjusted vision, we can see and understand all things. In Numbers chapters 13 and 14, ten of the twelve spies surveyed the giants and the walled cities from man's perspective. Caleb and Joshua, men of another spirit, regarded the same circumstances and strongholds through the eyes of the Lord.

The principle of Jesus' present priesthood emphasizes the difference between the Holy Place and the Most Holy Place, between a futuristic mentality and that which is at hand. The subject of the king-priest ministry of Jesus after the order of Melchisedec is treated thoroughly in the first chapter of *The More Excellent Ministry*. Suffice it to say here that His ministry flows in the present.

Everything Is in the Seed

Like the Old Covenant, the Feast of Pentecost is wholly futuristic in its outlook and scope. An outline of the whole Bible is an excellent illustration of this. One of the principal themes of the aggregate of Scripture is the Seed. To explain this, we must know that our Lord Jesus is especially represented by three Old Testament characters: Adam, Abraham and David. Jesus Christ is the Seed of the Woman, the Seed of Abraham and the Seed of David (Gen. 3:15; Matt. 1:1). Thus we see His pain, His power, and His promise as He relates to us racially (the Word made flesh), redemptively and royally. Below is an outline of the entire Bible. In the Word of God, we see that...

1. **The Seed comes.**
2. **The Seed dies.**
3. **The Seed lives.**
4. **The Seed speaks.**
5. **The Seed reigns.**

Gen. 3:15, KJV:

And I will put enmity between thee and the woman, and between thy seed and her seed; it shall bruise thy head, and thou shalt bruise his heel.

Gen. 3:15, NIV:

> *And I will put enmity between you and the woman, and between your offspring and hers; he will crush your head, and you will strike his heel.*

Throughout the Old Testament, from Genesis to Malachi, the message is clear: the Seed is coming! The Messiah was to be the Seed of the Woman who would destroy the works of the devil. To Moses, He was the mighty Prophet; to Isaiah, the Servant of Jehovah; to Malachi, the Messenger of the Covenant. The one message of the Old Testament is that the Seed is coming!

John 12:24, KJV:

> *Verily, verily, I say unto you, Except a corn of wheat fall into the ground and die, it abideth alone: but if it die, it bringeth forth much fruit.*

John 12:24, NIV:

> *I tell you the truth, unless a kernel of wheat falls to the ground and dies, it remains only a single seed. But if it dies, it produces many seeds.*

The Seed came, but He came to die! Matthew, Mark, Luke, and John all attest to His death. The Father planted the Son in the earth, that He might reap a family of sons in the image of the Firstborn (Rom. 8:29). This mighty harvest is the Church, the joy and expectation that was set before the Savior. In the Gospels, the Seed dies!

Acts 2:24, KJV:

...Whom God hath raised up, having loosed the pains of death: because it was not possible that he should be holden of it.

In the early Church, the Seed lives! The resurrection of the Lord Jesus was the keynote of the apostles' doctrine. The life of the risen Christ was the first concern of God for His infant Church. The baby had structure, but those bones were soft. Most importantly, the baby was alive, and its life was His life. In the Book of Acts, the Seed lives!

Heb. 1:1-2, KJV:

God, who at sundry times and in divers manners spake in time past unto the fathers by the prophets,

Hath in these last days spoken unto us by his Son, whom he hath appointed heir of all things, by whom also he made the worlds...

From Romans to Jude, the Seed speaks! Men such as Peter, Paul and John were among the literary apostles who gave us the letters of the New Testament. In them, we can hear the heart of Jesus, the Chief Apostle. Out of the abundance of His heart, He has spoken unto us. Throughout the epistles, the Seed speaks!

Rev. 11:15, KJV:

And the seventh angel sounded; and there were great voices in heaven, saying, The kingdoms of this world are become the kingdoms of our Lord, and of his Christ; and he shall reign for ever and ever.

In the Old Testament, the Seed is coming. In the Gospels, the Seed dies. In the Book of Acts, the Seed lives. In the epistles, the Seed speaks. And in the Revelation, the Seed reigns! He comes, He dies, He lives, He speaks, He reigns!

This panorama of Scripture also teaches how His life progressively unfolds within His people. We especially underscore the first point: in the Old Covenant, the Seed was ever coming. The religious order of His day loved Jesus so long as He was a prophecy; but when the Seed came and exposed their way of death by the manifestation of His life, the same teachers of prophecy crucified Him.

"It" Becomes "He"

The point is this: the Old Covenant was futuristic. Sadly, many today are proclaiming New Covenant realities with an Old Covenant spirit; that is to say, they are always looking to the future. To quickly balance this, men are raising the question, "Is the Kingdom of God now or future?" To that I emphatically answer, "Yes!" From the evangelicals waiting for an any-minute rapture to the sonship camp waiting for Romans 8:23, the fruit is the same: everyone is waiting for "it" to happen. Men argue vehemently over whether "it" is pre-, mid-, post-, or a-, and worship God in the restricted quarters of their own streams. The Father must chuckle as He looks from above to see His children's hands raised to praise Him, raised just high enough to clear the walls of their separate cubicles. Meanwhile, in the confines of that limited view, nobody ever takes the time to explain what "it" is. They are too busy feverishly declaring that "it" is coming!

Hab. 2:1-3, KJV:

I will stand upon my watch, and set me upon the tower, and will watch to see what he will say unto me, and what I shall answer when I am reproved.

And the Lord answered me, and said, Write the vision, and make it plain upon tables, that he may run that readeth it.

For the vision is yet for an appointed time, but at the end it shall speak, and not lie: though it tarry, wait for it; because it will surely come, it will not tarry.

Heb. 10:37, KJV:

For yet a little while, and he that shall come will come, and will not tarry.

While men of differing and sometimes conflicting opinions are waiting for "it" to happen, "He" has come! He is here, alive and well on planet earth. He is in His holy Temple, for God has sent forth the Spirit of His Son into our hearts (Gal. 4:6).

Most folks are waiting to do something great in the Kingdom of God. They talk about it, dream about it, wish for it. But nothing really happens in a man's life until he moves from an Old Covenant spirit to a New Covenant spirit, from a mindset that is future tense to one that acknowledges the God of the now.

Many already have the awareness of the indwelling Word and know that He has come, but they still linger in the death principle of that Seed. Wake up, saints! How long does it take to say "Yes" to the Lord? Settle it now. Following Jesus is going to cost you everything. Go ahead and die. Let the Seed come alive in you, and then let Him speak and reign through you. Too many Spirit-filled Christians are waiting to be holy enough to be used of God. "One of these days I will go forth," they ever cry. You will accomplish nothing worshiping the god of "gonna." Arise and shine, for your light has come (Isa. 60:1).

The Comings of the Lord

"But, Brother Varner, what about the coming of the Lord? Don't you believe that He is coming?" Yes, I do. Others inquire, "But is His coming literal or spiritual?" To that I say, "Yes!" It's both. His coming is literal and spiritual, future and present. The crowd in the Holy Place can only see a future coming, so that's all they preach; in that sense, they move in an Old Covenant spirit that says, "He is coming." But the spirit of the New Covenant is that the Son is here and that He is speaking. To show this more clearly, it is significant that the Bible reveals His first coming to be both literal and spiritual.

John 1:14, NIV:

The Word became flesh and lived for a while among us. We have seen his glory, the glory of the one and only Son, who came from the Father, full of grace and truth.

Luke 2:11-12, NIV:

Today in the town of David a Savior has been born to you; he is Christ the Lord.

This will be a sign to you: You will find a baby wrapped in cloths and lying in a manger.

1 Tim. 3:16, NIV:

Beyond all question, the mystery of godliness is great: He appeared in a body, was vindicated by the Spirit, was seen by angels, was preached among the nations, was believed on in the world, was taken up in glory.

That's plain enough. God was manifested in the flesh, in a body that came from a virgin womb. He is Emmanuel, God with us. But what about His spiritual coming the first time?

John 14:16-18, NIV:

And I will ask the Father, and he will give you another Counselor to be with you forever—

the Spirit of truth. The world cannot accept him, because it neither sees him nor knows him. But you know him, for he lives with you and will be in you.

I will not leave you as orphans; I will come to you.

John 14:23, NIV:

Jesus replied, "If anyone loves me, he will obey my teaching. My Father will love him, and we will come to him and make our home with him."

Acts 2:1- 4, NIV:

When the day of Pentecost came, they were all together in one place.

Suddenly a sound like the blowing of a violent wind came from heaven and filled the whole house where they were sitting.

They saw what seemed to be tongues of fire that separated and came to rest on each of them.

All of them were filled with the Holy Spirit and began to speak in other tongues as the Spirit enabled them.

Gal. 4:6, NIV:

Because you are sons, God sent the Spirit of his Son into our hearts, the Spirit who calls out, "Abba, Father."

Col. 1:27, NIV:

To them God has chosen to make known among the Gentiles the glorious riches of this mystery, which is Christ in you, the hope of glory.

The Bible is explicit. He came the first time in the flesh. God wrapped Himself in humanity and then Mary wrapped Him in swaddling clothes. No wonder the angels were excited that night. That glorious moment was the first time that any of them had seen God! Jesus Christ, the image of the invisible God, did not take upon Himself the nature of angels, but that of the seed of Abraham, as He partook of flesh and blood (Heb. 2:14-18).

But God also came the first time in the Spirit. He did not leave His disciples as orphans. He came on the Day of Pentecost, and He comes every time a believer is filled with the Holy Ghost. The indwelling Christ in the midst of His people is no longer a mystery. The Spirit of the Son in us is a present reality.

His first coming was a seed form of His second coming. He came the first time in flesh, then Spirit. In the cycle of restoration, the order is reversed, and He comes the second time in Spirit, then flesh. Weigh the increase of glory in both realms. In the sphere of the Spirit, the Pentecostal infilling, which is the firstfruits of the Spirit and the earnest of our inheritance (Rom. 8:23, Eph. 1:13-14), consummates in the fulness of the Spirit during the Feast of Tabernacles (John 3:34). In the realm of the flesh, Baby Jesus in the manger becomes King Jesus in the air!

Both hermeneutics are correct, but incomplete without each other. To those who only see His coming as literal, we amen your literal view, but add that He has come in the Spirit as well. To those who only see His coming as spiritual, we amen your spiritual view, but add that He is God and can take any form He wants at any time He wants. His resurrection was bodily, and that is the basis of our hope for the redemption of the body. To these who only view His coming as spiritual is added this caution: don't stop holding the Head (Col. 1:15-19; 2:8-10, 19). When one does away with the literal Jesus, he usually does away with the literal devil. He then becomes his own Christ and his own devil, and is quickly snared in the metaphysical nightmare of his own introspection. Whatever view we hold, we must not see His coming as only future.

The Spirit of Fear Has Picked Our Pockets

Our emphasis must be the immediate. This Melchisedec Principle can be depicted in several ways. For example, "Now faith is . . . " (Heb. 11:1) Faith doesn't claim anything. Real faith — God's faith — possesses the land. Consider the many examples found in Matthew 13, where the King repeatedly said, "The Kingdom of Heaven is . . . " The most striking way to show you that His priesthood is present is to declare that Jesus was crucified between two thieves: the past and the future!

Matt. 27:38, KJV:

Then were there two thieves crucified with him, one on the right hand, and another on the left.

Luke 23:39-43, NIV:

One of the criminals who hung there hurled insults at him: "Aren't you the Christ? Save yourself and us!"

But the other criminal rebuked him. "Don't you fear God," he said, "since you are under the same sentence?

We are punished justly, for we are getting what our deeds deserve. But this man has done nothing wrong."

Then he said, "Jesus, remember me when you come into your kingdom. "

Jesus answered him, "I tell you the truth, today you will be with me in paradise."

The first thief represents the past. He was so hopelessly bound and condemned by his former life that he had no hope. The second thief denotes the future, for he only had a future concept of the Kingdom. The Man on the middle cross was the God of *today!* He was the same God who sent Moses into Egypt (Ex. 3:14), for Jesus affirmed again and again in John's Gospel, "I am . . ." When He answered Peter that night on the storm-tossed lake, "It is I," the Greek reads *ego eimi*, "I am!"

2 Tim. 1:7, NIV:

> *For God did not give us a spirit of timidity, but a spirit of power, of love and of self-discipline.*

The spirit of fear only works through the past and the future. God, who is love (I John 4:18), who lives in the ever-present now, can relate to neither. Fear comes up from the past to accuse us because of previous mistakes. It comes from the future to intimidate and harass. The priesthood of the Feast of Pentecost is marked by this latter kind of fear, the fear of the future.

The Old Testament word for "thief" is #1590 in *Strong's Concordance* and means "a stealer." It is rendered "to thieve or deceive." How ironic that the fear of deception can be deceiving. The Greek word for "thief" is *kleptes* (Strong's #2812) and means "a stealer." It is taken from the verb *klepto* which means "to filch." Webster defines "filch" as a verb meaning "steal or pilfer." As an archaic noun, a "filch" was "the act of stealing; a staff with a hook in one end used by thieves in snatching small articles."

Song 2:15, KJV:

> *Take us the foxes, the little foxes, that spoil the vines: for our vines have tender grapes.*

Col. 2:8, KJV:

> *Beware lest any man spoil you through philosophy and vain deceit, after the tradition of men, after the rudiments of the world, and not after Christ.*

Col. 2:8, NIV:

> *See to it that no one takes you captive through hollow and deceptive philosophy, which depends on human tradition and the basic principles of this world rather than on Christ.*

Jesus was crucified between two thieves. The past is a thief. The future is a thief. These rascals have picked our pockets. The past has stolen from us, having come to us through the spirit of fear, and using two filches:

1. *"Why?"*
2. *"How long?"*

If you have children, you already know that the answer to the first question is "because." The remedy for the other hook of the past is "It's up to you."

Jesus was crucified between two thieves. The past is a thief. The future is also a pickpocket, having come to us through the spirit of fear, armed and carrying two more filches:

1. *"What if?"*
2. *"How shall it be?"*

The principle could be developed further, but the point is made. To be totally futuristic in one's outlook is to be deceived and robbed by the spirit of fear. There is no future in the past, and the devil doesn't care what we believe, so long as it pertains to the future. There's something about a "now" priesthood that scares the hell out of him.

Chapter Seven

The Measure Principle

The Man in the Mirror Has One Eye

The priesthood is changing. In the last chapter we learned that the mind of Christ is geared to the present, not the future. This ministry is also moving out of duality and into simplicity, or singleness. This chapter deals with the Measure Principle, for the Church will mature and come to His measure in the Most Holy Place, the Feast of Tabernacles. We are all to be judged by that one "measure," literally "the portion" of His life.

Eph. 4:13, NIV:

> *...until we all reach unity in the faith and in the knowledge of the Son of God and become mature, attaining to the whole measure of the fullness of Christ.*

Rev. 11:1, NIV:

> *I was given a reed like a measuring rod and was told, "Go and measure the temple of God and the altar, and count the worshipers there...."*

Rev. 21:15, NIV:

> *The angel who talked with me had a measuring rod of gold to measure the city, its gates and its walls.*

This new priesthood is to come to the singleness of His measure. But what is duality? Webster defines it to mean "doubleness, the state of being double; twofold, consisting of two." In philosophy, dualism admits of two independent and mutually irreducible substances in any given domain. The Bible calls it double-mindedness.

James 1:5-8, NIV:

> *If any of you lacks wisdom, he should ask God, who gives generously to all without finding fault, and it will be given to him.*
>
> *But when he asks, he must believe and not doubt, because he who doubts is like a wave of the sea, blown and tossed by the wind.*
>
> *That man should not think he will receive anything from the Lord;*
>
> *he is a double-minded man, unstable in all he does.*

To be "double-minded" is to be, literally, "double-souled." *Weymouth's* translation says that such a one is "a man of two minds, undecided in every step he takes." *Beck* says that he is "half-hearted," and *The Amplified Bible* terms such a one "hesitating, dubious, irresolute; he is unstable and unreliable and uncertain about everything he thinks, feels, decides."

It would be helpful at this point to review the concept of the Man in the Mirror detailed in Chapter Seven of *The*

More Excellent Ministry. The "genesis face" ()
was also mentioned in Chapter Three of this vol.   .e
"natural face" or "the face of our birth" is the fac. of the
new nature. As the priesthood is changing, we are emphasizing God's righteousness, not man's sinfulness.
The Man in the mirror is the new man, and he has one
eye!

Acts 2:46, KJV:

> *And they, continuing daily with one accord in the
> temple, and breaking bread from house to house, did eat
> their meat with gladness and singleness of heart...*

Matt. 6:22, KJV:

> *The light of the body is the eye: if therefore thine eye
> be single, thy whole body shall be full of light.*

Herein is a great truth: our eye is to be single. In the
context of this part of the Constitution of the Kingdom,
the King was teaching His disciples about light, or the
understanding of life. He mentions the lilies of the field
being clothed and arrayed with glory. For later con-
sideration, remember that any Bible study concerning
garments or the changing of garments (Zech. 3) will lead
to the words of Paul and the subject of immortality and
the redemption of the body.

2 Cor. 5:1-5, NIV:

> *Now we know that if the earthly tent we live in is
> destroyed, we have a building from God, an eternal
> house in heaven, not built by human hands.*

Meanwhile we groan, longing to be clothed with our heavenly dwelling,

because when we are clothed, we will not be found naked.

For while we are in this tent, we groan and are burdened, because we do not wish to be unclothed but to be clothed with our heavenly dwelling, so that what is mortal may be swallowed up by life.

Now it is God who has made us for this very purpose and has given us the Spirit as a deposit, guaranteeing what is to come.

The Man in the mirror, the new man, has one eye. His heart is fixed. His vision, like that of the dove, is single. His focus is not on God and the devil, but on God alone. He walks a different path, having chosen the highway, the high calling to be his portion.

Job 28:7-8, KJV:

There is a path which no fowl knoweth, and which the vulture's eye hath not seen:

The lion's whelps have not trodden it, nor the fierce lion passed by it.

Job 28:7-8, NIV:

No bird of prey knows that hidden path, no falcon's eye has seen it.

Proud beasts do not set foot on it, and no lion prowls there.

Isa. 35:8-10, NIV:

And a highway will be there; it will be called the Way of Holiness. The unclean will not journey on it; it will be for those who walk in that Way; wicked fools will not go about on it.

No lion will be there, nor will any ferocious beast get up on it; they will not be found there. But only the redeemed will walk there,

and the ransomed of the Lord will return. They will enter Zion with singing; everlasting joy will crown their heads. Gladness and joy will overtake them, and sorrow and sighing will flee away.

The devil doesn't know about this walk in the Spirit, the ascended life. His whelps, the demons, cannot decipher this highway to Zion. The Greek word for "demon" is *daimon* and can be rendered "a knowing one." The only way to walk in victory over the intelligences of the world system is to be clothed with a higher Intelligence, and we have the Mind of Christ (I Cor. 2:16). We have been born from above, and Jesus is the Wisdom from above. The "high" calling of Philippians 3:12-14 is the "upward" calling. The ascended life is also the replaced life (Gal. 2:20). All these thoughts are summed up in the Most Holy Place, the realm of His life (John 14:6).

Doublemindedness Is Idolatry

But the Holy Place realm, the Feast of Pentecost, carries the badge of duality. Too many of the saints are playing a guessing game. "He loves me . . . He loves me not."

... the adolescence of a stagnant Pentecostal theology, chained to a traditional mindset, these poor souls have drafted themselves into the civil war of Romans seven, ever intimidated by their teachers and peers, yet greatly needing to enter into the sabbath rest of the Most Holy Place (Romans eight).

The key word here is *focus*. Similar words are "vision" and "emphasis." The Lord is adjusting our vision. An early portion of Isaiah's prophecy clearly shows this point.

Isa. 21:11-12, KJV:

The burden of Dumah. He calleth to me out of Seir, Watchman, what of the night? Watchman, what of the night?

The watchman said, The morning cometh, and also the night: if ye will inquire, inquire ye: return, come.

Someone asks, "Pastor Varner, are you a night preacher or a day preacher?" Yes, I am. Both. When folks ask me about the night, I tell them that the morning is coming . . . and also the night; but my focus and emphasis is the dawning of a new day. All the day preachers need to preach a little bit of night, and all the night preachers need to preach a whole lot of day.

Heb. 7:18-19, NIV:

The former regulation is set aside because it was weak and useless

(for the law made nothing perfect), and a better hope is introduced, by which we draw near to God.

Rom. 8:1-4, NIV:

Therefore, there is now no condemnation for those who are in Christ Jesus,

because through Christ Jesus the law of the Spirit of life set me free from the law of sin and death.

For what the law was powerless to do in that it was weakened by the sinful nature, God did by sending his own Son in the likeness of sinful man to be a sin offering. And so he condemned sin in sinful man,

in order that the righteous requirements of the law might be fully met in us, who do not live according to the sinful nature but according to the Spirit.

Now we come to the heart of the matter: the change of priesthood is a change of law (Heb. 7:12). The law of the Spirit of life in Christ Jesus has made us free from the law of sin and death. But what about the devil? What about the old man? What about two natures in the believer? The Feast of Weeks is weak, bogged down in the double vision of two primary areas:

1. *God and the devil.*
2. *The new man and the old man.*

Again, the key word is *focus.* We are not doing away with the devil. My King, my heavenly David, took care of him (Heb. 2:14-15, I John 3:8). There is a literal devil — a defeated one. Jesus stripped him of his power and kingdom. The devil is not the thief of John 10:10 (read John 8-10 for the whole story). Yet he remains a worthy adversary to those who do not know the Word. Give him place and he will swallow you and your family (Eph.

4:27, I Pet. 5:8). Stay on the highway, resist him, and he will flee from you. Some Christians preach and practice dualism; they talk as much or more about satan as about Jesus. Whatever a man thinks or talks about the most, he worships; his god is in his mind and his mouth. Let's think about Jesus. Let's talk about Jesus. Let's sing about Jesus. Let's preach a great big Jesus and a wee little devil! The priesthood is changing. In the Most Holy Place, the vision is not two, but one. We must emphasize the Lord.

Heb. 12:1-2, NIV:

Therefore, since we are surrounded by such a great cloud of witnesses, let us throw off everything that hinders and the sin that so easily entangles, and let us run with perseverance the race marked out for us.

Let us fix our eyes on Jesus, the author and perfecter of our faith, who for the joy set before him endured the cross, scorning its shame, and sat down at the right hand of the throne of God.

2 Cor. 4:1-4, NIV:

Therefore, since through God's mercy we have this ministry, we do not lose heart.

Rather, we have renounced secret and shameful ways; we do not use deception, nor do we distort the word of God. On the contrary, by setting forth the truth plainly we commend ourselves to every man's conscience in the sight of God.

And even if our gospel is veiled, it is veiled to those who are perishing.

*The god of this age has blinded the minds of un-
believers, so that they cannot see the light of the gospel
of the glory of Christ, who is the image of God.*

Christ is the image of God. Antichrist is any other
image. Duality is idolatry. To focus on any other image
is to worship another god. We become what we look at.
We become what we worship. The Feast of Pentecost is
characterized by dual imagery. To give the devil place
is to worship him. To acknowledge the old man is
idolatry.

Rom. 1:23, KJV:

*...And changed the glory of the uncorruptible God
into an image made like to corruptible man, and to
birds, and fourfooted beasts, and creeping things.*

Rom. 1:25, KJV:

*...Who changed the truth of God into a lie, and wor-
shipped and served the creature more than the Creator,
who is blessed for ever. Amen.*

The word for "changed" in verse 23 is *allasso* and
means "to make different, exchange." Men have exchanged Christ, the image and glory of God, for a
lesser image. The word for "changed" in verse 25 is
metallasso, an intensified form of the previous word.
Note also the definite article in verse 25. Men have emphatically exchanged *the truth* for *the lie*. There are only
two men on the planet: Adam and Christ, the old man
and the new man. Their nicknames are "the lie" and
"the Truth."

John 8:44-45, NIV:

> *You belong to your father, the devil, and you want to carry out your father's desire. He was a murderer from the beginning, not holding to the truth, for there is no truth in him. When he lies, he speaks his native language, for he is a liar and the father of lies.*
>
> *Yet because I tell the truth, you do not believe me!*

The Pharisees, blinded by their religious traditions, were by nature the "lies" that the devil had fathered. They not only taught lies, they were lies! The lie is that satan is alive and well on planet earth and that the old man is still alive. The truth is that Jesus has defeated the devil and the old man has been crucified with his affections and lusts. Those who stop at the Feast of Pentecost are not so sure. Being partakers of a mixture of the lie and the truth, they can't make up their minds.

Gal. 2:20-21, KJV:

> *I am crucified with Christ: nevertheless I live; yet not I, but Christ liveth in me: and the life which I now live in the flesh I live by the faith of the Son of God, who loved me, and gave himself for me.*
>
> *I do not frustrate the grace of God: for if righteousness come by the law, then Christ is dead in vain.*

Gal. 2:20-21, NIV:

> *I have been crucified with Christ and I no longer live, but Christ lives in me. The life I live in the body, I live by faith in the Son of God, who loved me and gave himself for me.*

I do not set aside the grace of God, for if righteousness could be gained through the law, Christ died for nothing!

The New Testament in Basic English says, "I have been put to death on the cross with Christ." *The Amplified Bible* notes that we "have shared His crucifixion." *Young's Literal* agrees that "with Christ I have been crucified." *Phillip's* powerfully states, "I died on the cross with Christ!" The verb here is perfect passive indicative, first person singular. It is *sunestauromai*, "I have been crucified." The perfect tense in the Greek language shows action that has been completed in the past with ongoing results in the present. It is a combination of the past and the present, and expresses continuation from the past to the present time, or to the present of the speaker or writer, or else the result. Thus, "I have been crucified and remain crucified up until this present time." The identical verb is used one other place in Paul's writings.

Rom. 6:6, KJV:

Knowing this, that our old man is crucified with him, that the body of sin might be destroyed, that henceforth we should not serve sin.

Rom. 6:6, NIV:

For we know that our old self was crucified with him so that the body of sin might be rendered powerless, that we should no longer be slaves to sin...

All the verbs in the sixth chapter of Romans are perfect or aorist. The aorist tense expresses an action or event rounded off and complete in itself. It is a point in the expanse of time, whether in the past, the present, or the future, but especially in the past. Aorist is the "snapshot" tense, showing something that happened at a definite point of time.

Rom. 6:1-8, NIV:

What shall we say, then? Shall we go on sinning so that grace may increase?

By no means! We died to sin; how can we live in it any longer?

Or don't you know that all of us who were baptized into Christ Jesus were baptized into his death?

We were therefore buried with him through baptism into death in order that, just as Christ was raised from the dead through the glory of the Father, we too may live a new life.

If we have been united with him in his death, we will certainly also be united with him in his resurrection.

For we know that our old self was crucified with him so that the body of sin might be rendered powerless, that we should no longer be slaves to sin—

because anyone who has died has been freed from sin.

Now if we died with Christ, we believe that we will also live with him.

This space will not permit a verse-by-verse exegesis of Romans six, but the Word of God is unequivocal: The old man is dead! Furthermore, as one studies the epistles, he is hard pressed to find two natures in the believer. Those who have been genuinely born from above are dominated by one nature. Our problem is that we are fighting a memory (Isa. 26:13-14). The old man's picture is on the dresser and his socks are in the drawer, but he's dead! For a fuller and clearer treatment of the death of the old man, review the second chapter of *The More Excellent Ministry*.

A Just Measure

II Cor. 11:1-3, KJV:

Would to God ye could bear with me a little in my folly: and indeed bear with me.

For I am jealous over you with godly jealousy: for I have espoused you to one husband, that I may present you as a chaste virgin to Christ.

But I fear, lest by any means, as the serpent beguiled Eve through his subtilty, so your minds should be corrupted from the simplicity that is in Christ.

The priesthood is changing, and a ministry is moving on from duality to simplicity. The word of truth is delivering us from the perverted wisdom of the serpent. God hates mixture. He despises a diverse measure. When men focus on both God and the devil, on both the new man and the old man, they have to use a diverse measure. This affects and taints their every judgment.

Deut. 25:15, KJV:

But thou shalt have a perfect and just weight, a perfect and just measure shalt thou have: that thy days may be lengthened in the land which the Lord thy God giveth thee.

Deut. 25:15, NIV:

You must have accurate and honest weights and measures, so that you may live long in the land the Lord your God is giving you.

Micah 6:10, KJV:

Are there yet the treasures of wickedness in the house of the wicked, and the scant measure that is abominable?

The Hebrew word for "scant" here comes from a root which means "to emaciate, to make thin." It is rendered as "famish, or to wax lean" in the English Bible. To emaciate is to cause something to waste away. God wants an accurate measure in our hearts. He wants our lives, our homes, and our local churches to be healthy, not emaciated. His purpose is to conform us to the image of His Son. The reason we have a Baptist Jesus, a Pentecostal Jesus and a Kingdom Jesus is that men want to conform God to their image; they want God to change to accommodate their denominational opinions and doctrinal whims.

The decade of the 1990s has begun, and there is not a man, a message, a method or a movement in the earth that has a corner on what God is presently saying and doing. Every camp has sinned and come short of the glory of God. An emerging priesthood has yet to declare Jesus to be all that He is; this alone can be the model of our transformation, the measure of His life.

Deut. 22:9-11, NIV:

Do not plant two kinds of seed in your vineyard; if you do, not only the crops you plant but also the fruit of the vineyard will be defiled.

Do not plow with an ox and a donkey yoked together.

Do not wear clothes of wool and linen woven together.

The examples and illustrations of the Measure Principle are many. The reason is obvious: God wants all men to know the importance of the purity of the Seed. This will readily become apparent in our next chapter as we take the changing of the priesthood into the domestic realm.

Chapter Eight

The Marriage Principle

Authority and Submission Are Under the Curse

The good news of a changing priesthood is especially needed in the homes of America. We are moving from the future to the present in our perspective; we are pressing toward the mark of His one measure; now we must flow out of two wills into His one will. This is the Marriage Principle, for the husband-wife relationship must move beyond the veil. There is a covenantal walk for men and women in the Most Holy Place.

Because the Marriage Principle parallels the home and the local church throughout this chapter, it would be good to review God's two institutions as well as the principle of father's love and mother's love. These thoughts were covered in the beginning of chapter three of *The More Excellent Ministry*. There is an order of authority in God's two institutions:

THE HOME	THE LOCAL CHURCH
Jesus Christ	Jesus Christ
The man (husband/father)	The senior pastor/set man
The woman (wife/mother)	The other elders and deacons
The children	The saints

A man and a woman rightly related reveal the image of God, the love of God. "Mother's love" is always accepting, though acceptance does not necessarily mean approval. It is unconditional, free of requirements. Balance this with the firmness of "father's love," an earned respect that will not let the children have their way.

Because the subtitle of this chapter is so revealing, let us draw from words clearly expressed in *The More Excellent Ministry* concerning our transition from two wills in the Holy Place to one will in the Most Holy Place. This section has to do with a ministry without prejudice; in particular, the walls between men and women.

> *The second kind of prejudice is sexual. This is the battle of the sexes, the walls and fears that exist between men and women. . . . .*
>
> *I remember the early 1970s when it seemed like all we preached was church government and divine order. A fresh wave of that is in the land under different brands and handles. I'm glad for that, but I want to beseech you in this area. The "discipleship controversy" evolved because men, husbands in the home and shepherds in the local church, went too far. The extremes of authority and submission have gone beyond the limits to play God with people's lives. The whole*

principle of authority and submission is not to be an end in and of itself. It is, rather, to be a glorious means to an even more glorious end. This is a shocker, but did you know this truth?

All authority and submission is under the curse....

What? Yes, you heard me right. It wasn't until after the fall of man that the husband was to rule over the wife (Gen. 3:16). Prior to the fall, they were one. There was no need for authority and submission; it was swallowed up in simplicity and union. In order for authority and submission to operate, there must be two wills. One will must come under and submit to the other will. For that reason, we see that obedience is not the ultimate goal. There is something greater than my submitting to His will. The highest order of anything is to become it! We are to come into union with His will . . . one will. Jesus was the Pattern for this. He who was rich became poor. The Word was made flesh. He condescended from the realm of perfect order and worship to the lower realm of death and chaos. He identified with broken humanity, and, as such, lowered Himself into a relationship of authority and submission to the Father. Prior to that, He and the Father were one. He lowered Himself even further and submitted to Joseph and Mary, and to the law.

Now, lest you think that I am belittling the truth of authority and submission, let me state that this was the only principle by which Jesus Christ walked out from under the curse, bringing us up and out with Him! We were in His loins. So I preach and practice government.... I still pastor a local church. I've seen both sides of the coin. On the one hand, men teach that authority and submission are all-important; others are teaching that authority and submission are not important at all. Guess where the truth is? The first crowd is killing folks with legalism; the other is killing folks quicker with license. Paul dealt with both issues in his letter to the Galatians, showing us that law and lust will abort the seed of God. [But we must keep all of this in proper perspective. The ascension-gift ministries are "until . . ." They are passing, not permanent. Again, they are the means to an end, not the end. They are but a vehicle and a tool to bring us to a higher purpose: union with Him within the veil.]

Submission does not denote inferiority. The man is not better or smarter than the woman. There are wonderful differences. For example, men are headliners and women are fine printers. If the woman is the weaker vessel, then the man is the weak vessel (I Pet. 3:1-7).... a man and a woman rightly related reveal the image of God. It takes both. Two become one. There is a place of perfect union where that which is in part shall be done away. I know that the local church is a shadow of that reality. I am aware of what the "deeper life" teachers are saying...I also know that we haven't arrived. The experience of Ephesians 4:13 is still ahead of us. Some may read this and self-destruct. "Praise God, I'm free! I submit to no man," is the banner of a wild man. But we still need husbands in the home and pastors in the church. Let us follow the Leader. Jesus arrived at full stature by tasting fully of submission to the will of the Father.

The More Excellent Ministry, pp. 115-117

Only the Holy Ghost can write this truth upon your heart. The 80s gave us what could be called a neo-discipleship move. In the 70s, God brought some much-needed order to the Charismatic renewal. In the last ten years, He began to do the same among the faith churches. Both times have seen excesses in local and translocal authority. We need a fresh perspective; we need a change of attitude in the priesthood. So God is moving us from the strain of two wills to the sabbath rest of one will. In the home and the local church, the Marriage Principle is at work.

Three Kingdom Principles of Authority

Many of you have been burned, abused by preachers and other people. This is a hard truth, but God has always given you the kind of ministry that you needed, even though some were badger-skin coverings, very rough. There is a great need in the international community to clarify this entire subject of authority and submission.

There are three basic principles of authority in the Kingdom of God.

1. *All authority centers in Jesus.*
2. *Authority is never enforced, only recognized.*
3. *Authority can only work through personal relationships.*

First, it must be understood that all authority centers in Jesus Christ. All authority, whether domestic, ecclesiastical or civil, is delegated authority . . . His authority.

Matt. 28:18-20, NIV:

Then Jesus came to them and said, "All authority in heaven and on earth has been given to me.

> *Therefore go and make disciples of all nations, baptizing them in the name of the Father and of the Son and of the Holy Spirit,*
>
> *and teaching them to obey everything I have commanded you. And surely I will be with you always, to the very end of the age."*

All authority is His authority. I don't have any. Neither do you. The One who divided the five loaves on the earth divided Himself into five loaves when He ascended. Jesus is the Apostle, the Prophet, the Evangelist, the Pastor and the Teacher (Eph. 4:11).

Heb. 3:1, KJV:

> *Wherefore, holy brethren, partakers of the heavenly calling, consider the Apostle and High Priest of our profession, Christ Jesus...*

Acts 3:22-23, KJV:

> *For Moses truly said unto the fathers, A prophet shall the Lord your God raise up unto you of your brethren, like unto me; him shall ye hear in all things whatsoever he shall say unto you.*
>
> *And it shall come to pass, that every soul, which will not hear that prophet, shall be destroyed from among the people.*

Luke 4:18, KJV:

> *The Spirit of the Lord is upon me, because he hath anointed me to preach the gospel to the poor; he hath sent me to heal the brokenhearted, to preach deliverance to the captives, and recovering of sight to the blind, to set at liberty them that are bruised...*

John 10:11, KJV:

I am the good shepherd: the good shepherd giveth his life for the sheep.

John 3:2, KJV:

The same came to Jesus by night, and said unto him, Rabbi, we know that thou art a teacher come from God: for no man can do these miracles that thou doest, except God be with him.

Jesus was and is all five ministries. Much more will be said about Jesus the Prophet in the next chapter. The Head of the Church has been given all executive authority in Heaven and in earth. His Name is higher than any other.

Secondly, every leader must understand that authority is never enforced; it is only recognized and acknowledged.

1. *All authority centers in Jesus.*
2. *Authority is never enforced, only recognized.*
3. *Authority can only work through personal relationships.*

Tit. 1:1, KJV:

Paul, a servant of God, and an apostle of Jesus Christ, according to the faith of God's elect, and the acknowledging of the truth which is after godliness...

If a husband in the home, a pastor in the church, or an extralocal ministry in the churches has to bully people, his "authority" may not be genuine. Psychic manipulation, fear tactics and intimidation have no place in the life of the believer or the house of the Lord. The

earlier years of most ministries saw such occasional out-
bursts of immaturity, but Jesus has forgiven those of us
who have repented.

The local church is autonomous; that is, it is self-
governing, self-propagating and self-reproducing.
Under Jesus Christ, the Head of the Church, there is no
higher authority on the planet, and there is no court of
appeals. The grandest truth of the New Covenant is the
rent veil. There are three entities which are sovereign,
made in the image of a Sovereign God:

1. *The will of an individual.*
2. *The home.*
3. *The local church.*

No one will care about how much we know until he
knows how much we care. One is completely out of order
when he pushes his way into a person's heart. If an individual doesn't want ministry, we are helpless; there is
nothing we can do or say. It is a sin to browbeat and drive
the sheep. But how sad it is that some saints won't blow their
nose without their shepherd's consent. The result of all this
bondage is immature sheep and burned-out shepherds.

There are many areas of married life that are
sacrosanct. This holy ground is nobody else's business,
off limits to all but the husband and wife. All marital conflicts must be eventually healed from the inside out if the
reconciliation is to remain. Many couples are snared in
the bondage of having to get permission to do what God
deems sacred to their private domain.

Foundational ministries, apostles and prophets, need
to learn again how to be servant-leaders to the churches.

We must be sent under authority and be willing to submit to local eldership. Some local churches are afraid to breathe without their "apostle" knowing all about it. A real apostle will not make the saints depend on him; he will eventually work himself out of a job.

All authority centers in Jesus. Authority is never bossy; it is only recognized as it serves.

Thirdly, authority can only work through personal relationships.

1. *All authority centers in Jesus.*
2. *Authority is never enforced, only recognized.*
3. *Authority can only work through personal relationships.*

John 19:34, KJV:

> *But one of the soldiers with a spear pierced his side, and forthwith came there out blood and water.*

Lev. 17:11, KJV:

> *For the life of the flesh is in the blood: and I have given it to you upon the altar to make an atonement for your souls: for it is the blood that maketh an atonement for the soul.*

Authority produces relationships. This is demonstrated by the principle of blood and water. Because Jesus shed His blood for me, He has a legal right to wash my feet (John 13:1-17). He suffered and laid down His life for me; on that basis, He has a legal right to speak into my life. The abuses of authority already mentioned are inevitable where men and women are ignorant of this principle.

I have every right to correct my four children, for I have shed blood for each of them. I have every right to speak into the lives of the people in my church because I have laid down my time, talent and treasure for them. As an extralocal ministry, I experience all kinds of situations in different churches. When operating in the prophetic ministry, I see a great need for adjustments in many lives, especially those of leaders. But until I shed some blood for a local pastor, I am reluctant to speak to those situations. Once a relationship is realized, my words will be far more effective, even life-changing. That's better than a worn-out hair-trigger on a prophecy gun.

There is a flip side to this third principle. My wife Joann often speaks powerfully into my life because she has shed blood for me and with me for over eighteen years. Charlie Baird and Nat Rand, two of my closest friends and also elders in our local assembly, have walked with me for years through many experiences, good, bad and even ugly. When they have something to say to me, I listen. There are apostles and prophets all over this great nation who have spoken into my life, but these men and women love me. I am in touch with them all the time. We have shed blood and laid down our lives for each other and our churches. I don't let just anyone speak into my life. Neither should you.

There are exceptions to every principle. I have prophesied the Word of the Lord to complete strangers. But, as a principle of ministry, I want to give of my life to a person first; then I can have real liberty and confidence to speak to his heart. Only then my words will have clout.

The Sons of the Prophets

The consequence of government is relationship. This third Kingdom principle of authority needs further illustration. The principle of authority operating through relationships is uniquely illustrated in the Old Testament settings of the "company" of the prophets under Samuel and the "sons" of the prophets under Elijah and Elisha. (For what it's worth, the term "school of the prophets" is not in the Bible.)

I Sam. 10:5, KJV:

> *After that thou shalt come to the hill of God, where is the garrison of the Philistines: and it shall come to pass, when thou art come thither to the city, that thou shalt meet a company of prophets coming down from the high place with a psaltery, and a tabret, and a pipe, and a harp, before them; and they shall prophesy.*

I Sam. 19:19-20, KJV:

> *And it was told Saul, saying, Behold, David is at Naioth in Ramah.*
>
> *And Saul sent messengers to take David: and when they saw the company of the prophets prophesying, and Samuel standing as appointed over them, the spirit of God was upon the messengers of Saul, and they also prophesied.*

1 Sam. 8:1-5, NIV:

> *When Samuel grew old, he appointed his sons as judges for Israel.*
>
> *The name of his firstborn was Joel and the name of his second was Abijah, and they served at Beersheba.*

> *But his sons did not walk in his ways. They turned aside after dishonest gain and accepted bribes and perverted justice.*
>
> *So all the elders of Israel gathered together and came to Samuel at Ramah.*
>
> *They said to him, "You are old, and your sons do not walk in your ways; now appoint a king to lead us, such as all the other nations have."*

Samuel was a powerful man and one of the greatest prophets in the Bible. However, these verses clearly show that he did not take time to build a relationship with his sons. He put them on staff because they were natural kin, not because they walked after him and his God (I Sam. 12:18). On account of this weakness, the young prophets who followed Samuel were at best a "company," not a family. The word for "company" in chapter 10 means "a rope; a company (as if tied together)"; the word for "company" in chapter 19 means "to gather, an assembly." What began as a relationship degenerated into prophesying contests several times a week.

Samuel made the same mistake with his spiritual sons as he had with Joel and Abijah. Perhaps he had learned this folly from Eli (I Sam. 2:22-25, 3:11-13). Samuel loved God, but he lived in a place called *Ramah*, "a high place, height, an elevation, an exaltation, a sublimity." Was this prophet proud, or just caught up in his national ministry? May God pour mercy on us who have failed to learn from Samuel's ignorance: he was a powerful prophet but not a wise father . . . a preacher, but not a pastor.

II Kings 2:3, KJV:

And the sons of the prophets that were at Bethel came forth to Elisha, and said unto him, Knowest thou that the Lord will take away thy master from thy head today? And he said, Yea, I know it; hold ye your peace.

II Kings 2:5, KJV:

And the sons of the prophets that were at Jericho came to Elisha, and said unto him, Knowest thou that the Lord will take away thy master from thy head today? And he answered, Yea, I know it; hold ye your peace.

II Kings 2:7, KJV:

And fifty men of the sons of the prophets went, and stood to view afar off: and they two stood by Jordan.

II Kings 2:15, KJV:

And when the sons of the prophets which were to view at Jericho saw him, they said, The spirit of Elijah doth rest on Elisha. And they came to meet him, and bowed themselves to the ground before him.

II Kings 4:1, KJV:

Now there cried a certain woman of the wives of the sons of the prophets unto Elisha, saying, Thy servant my husband is dead; and thou knowest that thy servant did fear the Lord: and the creditor is come to take unto him my two sons to be bondmen.

II Kings 4:38, KJV:

And Elisha came again to Gilgal: and there was a dearth in the land; and the sons of the prophets were sitting before him: and he said unto his servant, Set on the great pot, and see the pottage for the sons of the prophets.

II Kings 5:22, KJV:

And he said, All is well. My master hath sent me, saying, Behold, even now there be come to me from mount Ephraim two young men of the sons of the prophets: give them, I pray thee, a talent of silver, and two changes of garments.

II Kings 6:1, KJV:

And the sons of the prophets said unto Elisha, Behold now, the place where we dwell with thee is too strait for us.

A new day is dawning. Once again, people have become more important than things. The verses above afford much insight into the present-day condition of the prophetic ministry in this nation. Eight times the Bible mentions "the sons of the prophets." Eight is the number of a new beginning, and explains why men and women everywhere are now craving and crying out for relationships, not just giftings. Yet fifty prophets are content to stand afar off, fearing to pay the price of walking through Jordan with their mentors. Fifty is the number of Pentecost. Only the Elishas who move on to the Feast of Tabernacles receive the double portion, literally, "the portion of the firstborn."

Not long after Elijah's ascension, the "sons" of the prophets began to backslide into a "company" again; by the time of chapter four of Second Kings, one prophet had already died, indicted by the love of money, and his sons had become momma's boys. He had never prioritized enough time to minister to his family. Then came the famine in the land (Amos 8:11-14). In the face of this great need, the prophets were contentedly and comfortably sitting before their leader, ever learning more revelation knowledge so they could more impressively lay hands on each other. The land was dying, but they didn't care. No wonder there was death in the pot! Not long after, Elisha had to turn more and more to a new generation of younger men to get the job done, young men who were willing to walk the straight and narrow, young people who were more righteous than their fathers.

II Kings 9:1-3, KJV:

And Elisha the prophet called one of the children of the prophets, and said unto him, Gird up thy loins, and take this box of oil in thine hand, and go to Ramoth-gilead:

And when thou comest thither, look out there Jehu the son of Jehoshaphat the son of Nimshi, and go in, and make him arise up from among his brethren, and carry him to an inner chamber;

Then take the box of oil, and pour it on his head, and say, Thus saith the Lord, I have anointed thee king over Israel. Then open the door, and flee, and tarry not.

Finally, Elisha gave up on the "sons" who had become a "company" again, and commissioned one of the "grandsons" when the time came for prophets to anoint kings. What a picture! What a lesson! Authority only works through relationships; there is a mighty difference between the "company" of the prophets and the "sons" of the prophets.

Rom. 12:1-2, KJV:

I beseech you therefore, brethren, by the mercies of God, that ye present your bodies a living sacrifice, holy, acceptable unto God, which is your reasonable service.

And be not conformed to this world: but be ye transformed by the renewing of your mind, that ye may prove what is that good, and acceptable, and perfect, will of God.

There are not three wills of God. His one will is good, and acceptable, and perfect. We are moving from the Holy Place to the Most Holy Place, from the Feast of Pentecost to the Feast of Tabernacles. We are growing up from the realm of two wills, either trying to do His will or being dominated by another's will. We have entered the realm of becoming His will, moving up from obedience to union. Relationship with Him and the brethren is the key. As we continue to experience this changing of the priesthood, we must be alert . . . we must hear His voice.

Chapter Nine

The Mouthpiece Principle

Gathered by the Voice of One

This chapter, "The Mouthpiece Principle," is most relevant, and is tied to the preceding one, especially its concluding section on the sons of the prophets. We are hearing much about prophets and prophetesses these days. Indeed, men must hear the Word of the Lord, and God is speaking through His servants the prophets. However, the priesthood is changing, and we are shifting from the voice of the many to the Voice of the One, from the voice of the prophets to the Voice of the Son.

Amos 3:7, KJV:

Surely the Lord God will do nothing, but he revealeth his secret unto his servants the prophets.

Amos 3:7, NIV:

Surely the Sovereign Lord does nothing without revealing his plan to his servants the prophets.

This key verse teaches that the prophets do not make things happen; we only declare what His Majesty has determined to do. The Feast of Pentecost is marked by a company of prophets. The Feast of Tabernacles is the platform for *the* Prophet, the Lord Jesus Christ. The voices of the prophets are to be swallowed up in the Voice of the Son. We learned in Chapter Three about the changing of the covenants, the taking away of the Old Testament and the establishing of the New. Consider that truth again in light of the verses below. The prophets were the voices of the Old Covenant; the Son is the Voice of the New. That was then; this is now.

Heb. 1:1-2, KJV:

God, who at sundry times and in divers manners spake in time past unto the fathers by the prophets,

Hath in these last days spoken unto us by his Son, whom he hath appointed heir of all things, by whom also he made the worlds...

Heb. 1:1-2, NIV:

In the past God spoke to our forefathers through the prophets at many times and in various ways,

but in these last days he has spoken to us by his Son, whom he appointed heir of all things, and through whom he made the universe.

A prophet is God's mouthpiece, one who speaks for another. The Mouthpiece Principle is essential to a priesthood that is changing. All present-day vision for prophetic ministry must be kept in the perspective of God's ultimate purpose. Anything said herein that may adjust or seem to correct such vision is spoken with His view to the whole.

I move in the prophetic, including personal ministry. I have prophesied over many people in the last twenty years, collectively and individually. I have flowed in the realm of general or simple prophecy, that is, prophecy that edifies, exhorts and comforts, words which build up, stir up and cheer up (I Cor. 14:3). I have also moved jointly with other prophetic ministries in the realm of prediction, direction and judgment. (Please understand that I am not offering you my spiritual pedigree; I am only letting you know that I have experienced the prophetic ministry.) I live in the prophetic. The words that I speak or write jump in your spirit because of the life of God in both of us. Deep has to call to deep. Without the impartation and anointing of the Holy Ghost as He quickens the Word of God, I have nothing to say. Without the prophetic, I cannot live or minister, and you cannot hear.

The realm of the Prophet, the Son, is the realm of the Most Holy Place. There is something far greater than the world's foremost prophet laying hands on you and prophesying the Word of the Lord over your life: the Voice of Jesus Himself within your spirit!

This chapter might be a little rough on those who have an ego problem, men or women who must be center-stage, wanting to be seen and heard. Others who oppose the present-day prophetic move may think that I am in their corner, but they have often misunderstood God's words, too. Being led by their reason, these spiritual stoics need praying grandmas.

God is restoring the prophetic to the Church, but it must be held in the perspective of three dimensions, not just two. It is passing, not permanent. Like the issue of authority and submission, the prophetic is a vehicle, a means to an end, and not the end itself. The priesthood is changing, and the streams of the prophets must flow into one river, the Voice of the Son.

Moses the prophet is a good illustration. The children of Israel were content to let the man of God go up the mountain and talk to the Lord; while Moses heard for them, they rose up and played. Many today are immature and irresponsible, compassing land and sea, drooling for a "word." Prophecy is precious. We do not make light of those of you who really need to hear from the Lord, but we are declaring how you are to survive the next ten years: you must learn to hear the Voice of Jesus for yourself! The purpose of every godly parent, pastor or prophet is that those under their care learn to pray and listen for the Voice of the Lord. In the Old Testament, only Moses and the elders climbed the mountain. In the New Testament, because of a rent veil, each of us, all of us, can go up the mountain!

Eph. 2:18, KJV:

> *For through him we both have access by one Spirit unto the Father.*

The Hearing Ear

Prov. 20:12, KJV:

> *The hearing ear, and the seeing eye, the Lord hath made even both of them.*

In the spring of 1989, the Lord spoke powerfully in my spirit and said, "I am sovereignly opening the ears of my people. I am creating the hearing ear." From that time until now, I have witnessed firsthand in this nation, from one coast to the other, an unprecedented hunger for the things of the Spirit. Men are tired of peanuts, popcorn and candy. They are ready to hear and to feed on present truth.

One of the greatest needs in the American church is for expository preachers of the Bible, men and women full of the Holy Ghost who will faithfully exegete the Scriptures. The sheep need more than clever slogans and cliches backed up with a few scattered proof texts. We must feed the sheep by preaching the Word. The most important thing the Lord is doing right now is opening the eyes and the ears of His people. The eyes of the heart (Eph. 1:18) and the ears of the inner man are beginning to come alive at the sound of the Voice of One.

Eph. 2:6, KJV:

...And hath raised us up together, and made us sit together in heavenly places in Christ Jesus...

Ezek. 34:11-16, NIV:

For this is what the Sovereign Lord says: I myself will search for my sheep and look after them.

As a shepherd looks after his scattered flock when he is with them, so will I look after my sheep. I will rescue them from all the places where they were scattered on a day of clouds and darkness.

I will bring them out from the nations and gather them from the countries, and I will bring them into their own land. I will pasture them on the mountains of Israel, in the ravines and in all the settlements in the land.

I will tend them in a good pasture, and the mountain heights of Israel will be their grazing land. There they will lie down in good grazing land, and there they will feed in a rich pasture on the mountains of Israel.

I myself will tend my sheep and have them lie down, declares the Sovereign Lord.

I will search for the lost and bring back the strays. I will bind up the injured and strengthen the weak, but the sleek and the strong I will destroy. I will shepherd the flock with justice.

Ezek. 34:23, KJV:

And I will set up one shepherd over them, and he shall feed them, even my servant David; he shall feed them, and he shall be their shepherd.

John 10:14, KJV:

I am the good shepherd, and know my sheep, and am known of mine.

John 10:4-5, NIV:

When he has brought out all his own, he goes on ahead of them, and his sheep follow him because they know his voice.

But they will never follow a stranger; in fact, they will run away from him because they do not recognize a stranger's voice.

Acts 9:7, KJV:

And the men which journeyed with him stood speechless, hearing a voice, but seeing no man.

Rom. 10:17, NIV:

Consequently, faith comes from hearing the message, and the message is heard through the word of Christ.

Ps. 50:5, NIV:

Gather to me my consecrated ones, who made a covenant with me by sacrifice.

Meditate on these verses. As the priesthood is being changed, there is a gathering unto One by the Voice of One. It is not the voice of two, but the Voice of One. Every man and woman who has been gifted with the prophetic spirit, the Elijah spirit, needs to say with John the Baptist, "I am the voice of one . . ."

Matt. 3:1-3, KJV:

In those days came John the Baptist, preaching in the wilderness of Judaea,

And saying, Repent ye: for the kingdom of heaven is at hand.

For this is he that was spoken of by the prophet Esaias, saying, The voice of one crying in the wilderness, Prepare ye the way of the Lord, make his paths straight.

Isa. 40:3-5, KJV:

The voice of him that crieth in the wilderness, Prepare ye the way of the Lord, make straight in the desert a highway for our God.

Every valley shall be exalted, and every mountain and hill shall be made low: and the crooked shall be made straight, and the rough places plain:

And the glory of the Lord shall be revealed, and all flesh shall see it together: for the mouth of the Lord hath spoken it.

Who was this man? Not Prophet John, but the voice of Him who cries. The mouth of the Lord is the many-membered Voice of Him. His Voice is causing a gathering, a bundling, an assembling. We are being gathered by the Voice of One. Along with this, note that the promises of God were not made to the many, but to the One (Gal. 3:16). Everywhere today, men are gathering. But to what and why? Men gather to many things for many reasons.

This gathering together unto Him is taking place in the heavenlies before it is taking place in the earth; it is taking place in the Spirit as we hear Him. Only then can we learn of Him and be measured by Him. This is not a roundup, but a gathering together. The issue here is not His union with us, but our union with Him. He became us that we might become Him (II Cor. 5:17-21). This union with Him can only happen in the Most Holy Place. Togetherness is the way it is there. Until now, we have been members not yet a body and stones not yet a house; we have been disjointed, separated, a valley of dry bones (Ezek. 37). Men have tried to put us together, but there has been no genuine gathering. Unity cannot be created; it can only be kept, for all unity is essentially based on the unity between the Father and the Son and these seven absolutes:

Eph. 4:4-6, KJV:

There is one body, and one Spirit, even as ye are called in one hope of your calling;

One Lord, one faith, one baptism,

One God and Father of all, who is above all, and through all, and in you all.

Body, Soul, and Spirit

What is this gathering all about? Better asked, what is this gathering *not* all about? First of all, this gathering is not taking place in the realm of the body, the natural, the flesh. The first Adam was made of dirt. When he fell, we all lost the sound of God's voice. Men are gathering in this first arena. In the world, they gather to fame, sex, sports and what money can buy. Every weekend in America, men gather in the realm of dirt, the realm of Adam. Remember, too, that in the world there are many voices, but in the Kingdom, there is but one Voice, the Voice of Him.

I Cor. 14:10, KJV:

There are, it may be, so many kinds of voices in the world, and none of them is without signification.

The Holy Place is cluttered with the kingdoms of the many; the Most Holy Place is the Kingdom of the One.

His gathering is not taking place in the world, neither the secular world, nor the religious world.

In the religious world of the natural realm, men are gathering for various reasons. Believe it or not, in this country there are still "white" churches and "black" churches. The only reason some men gather around issues and causes is because of race. We are not gathering unto white or black, nor are we gathering unto a mingling of white and black. Others gather unto a building. That, too, is dirt. It isn't dirty to have a building or meet in a building (some get their kicks by kicking that horse); but we are not gathering unto a building. Men worship their facilities, never having understood that the building, however ornate, is only a sheepshed, the place where the Building meets (I Cor. 3:9-11). Then folks say, "After you get into our building, you should hear our choir! Oh, what music! We have the best musicians in town." But praise isn't music. They persist, "And you must come and hear our preacher! He's the best we've ever heard." But the Day of the Lord has dawned, and the day of our gathering around a man or a personality, our favorite preacher, is over. There is no idolatry in the Most Holy Place.

What a pile of dirt! Adam was made of dirt. Pour water on dirt, and all you get is mud. Earth, dust, the flesh, the natural, the serpent's meat (Gen. 3:14, Isa. 65:25) . . . hear the truth of this, don't just see the semantics; we are being gathered unto One by the Voice of One, and we are moving from the prophets to the Son.

There are different kinds of dirt: famous dirt, sexy dirt, athletic dirt, expensive dirt, white dirt, black dirt, brick and stone dirt, talented dirt, eloquent dirt . . . but they are all still dirt. And every kind of dirt has its own advocate or mouthpiece, a veritable zoo of carnival barkers clamoring for the souls of men (Rev. 18:13). Hear the chant of the moneychangers, "Step right up, sir. It will only cost you your life."

So how do we deal with it all? God already has. His remedy for Adam and his nature of mixture was the cross. Nothing listed above is a Scriptural reason for gathering. Jesus is tipping the tables of the money-changers; the King is cleansing the Temple, and the devil has nothing to eat. Our Lord in His death cancelled the dirt pile, the dunghill, and in His resurrection has lifted His royal priesthood (I Sam. 2:8) up and out of that into a higher calling and drawing.

Body . . . soul. Secondly, we are not being gathered in the realm of the soul, or mind. This may shock you, but we are not being gathered unto knowledge or unto a message, even the "Kingdom message." Eve reached for knowledge and the heavens closed. Knowing "the message" is not where it's at. Paul didn't want to know "the message"; Paul wanted to know *Him* (Phil. 3:7-11).

Those who gather in soul only want information. Some of you picked up this book for that reason: more sermon material. But information must become il-lumination. You need some light on the subject. Then illumination becomes inspiration. You've got to have it. Inspiration will bring you to revelation as you see Him. Then revelation must become realization. It must be real in your spirit. This realization will cause a transformation in your lifestyle. Only then will there be a manifestation of the Christ-life in and through you, and everyone will know it because they can see it. Mere information is a far cry from manifestation.

Information (or the lack of it) leads to separation and, coupled with the wrong spirit, causes mutilation. Jesus taught us to build our lives and ministries on the rock and not the sand. Sand is but particles of rock. To build on the sand is to build on part of the Rock, on one emphasis or doctrine, rather than on Him who is the Sum of all things.

Each one of those sandy particles has its own group of "party prophets." When men gather to partial knowledge, they gather into groups based on maturity levels and prophesy to each other. Just look in the yellow pages; we're so classified that we can't learn from each other. Across the nation, men are gathering to a message, to knowledge. Listen and you will hear "prophets" in every one of those sometimes warring camps saying "Thus saith the Lord." Many voices. I don't want to add still another voice to this shouting match, but everybody can't be right. Maybe you're asking, "O.K., Varner, who is right?" *He is.*

His priesthood is not being gathered in the realm of soul, mind or intellect. We are not being gathered unto knowledge, nor are we being gathered unto experiences. The American church is very experience-oriented. We have been governed by impulse and not principle, by our feelings and not the Word of God, walking after the flesh and not after the Spirit. Men are always asking, "Have you experienced the new birth? Have you received the Holy Ghost since you believed? Have you stepped through the rent veil?" Whatever the tag, and no matter how valid and meaningful the experience was and is, we are not being gathered to an experience. The realm of the soul, like the realm of the body, is to be dealt with by the cross of Christ. It must be crucified until it doesn't even think that it might be the One. It must be killed, nailed to His cross.

Gen. 49:10, KJV:

> *The sceptre shall not depart from Judah, nor a lawgiver from between his feet, until Shiloh come; and unto him shall the gathering of the people be.*

Gen. 49:10, NIV:

> *The scepter will not depart from Judah, nor the ruler's staff from between his feet, until he comes to whom it belongs and the obedience of the nations is his.*

Body . . . soul . . . spirit. The gathering of which we speak is in the realm of spirit. It is in the realm of the Christ, the Son. We are being gathered unto One by the Voice of One. We are being gathered unto a Person, unto Him! Everything is being reduced and simplified into Him. We must hear Him, see Him, walk after Him, become like Him. We must be gathered unto Him!

Song 1:4, KJV:

> *Draw me, we will run after thee: the king hath brought me into his chambers: we will be glad and rejoice in thee, we will remember thy love more than wine: the upright love thee.*

Song 1:4, NIV:

Take me away with you—let us hurry! The king has brought me into his chambers. We rejoice and delight in you; we will praise your love more than wine. How right they are to adore you!

Eph. 1:9-10, KJV:

Having made known unto us the mystery of his will, according to his good pleasure which he hath purposed in himself:

That in the dispensation of the fulness of times he might gather together in one all things in Christ, both which are in heaven, and which are on earth; even in him...

Eph. 1:9-10, NIV:

And he made known to us the mystery of his will according to his good pleasure, which he purposed in Christ,

to be put into effect when the times will have reached their fulfillment—to bring all things in heaven and on earth together under one head, even Christ.

The Inward Urgency of the Kingdom

This is the day of gathering. We are being summoned by the Voice of One. The blowing of the trumpets, the prophets of the Lord, are bringing a certain sound, the sound of His calling.

Rom. 8:28-30, NIV:

And we know that in all things God works for the good of those who love him, who have been called according to his purpose.

For those God foreknew he also predestined to be conformed to the likeness of his Son, that he might be the firstborn among many brothers.

And those he predestined, he also called; those he called, he also justified; those he justified, he also glorified.

Rom. 11:29, NIV:

...for God's gifts and his call are irrevocable.

Eph. 4:1, NIV:

As a prisoner for the Lord, then, I urge you to live a life worthy of the calling you have received.

Heb. 5:4, NIV:

No one takes this honor upon himself; he must be called by God, just as Aaron was.

We are the called according to His purpose. In Romans 11:29, note that the *charismata* are plural, but the calling (there is a definite article) is singular—one calling. It is also genitive; *ou theou* denotes origin and character. This calling is out of Him and marked by Him. Having walked through the turmoil of the 1980s, it is good to know that there are three things about His calling that never change:

1. *The Person who called you.*

   Heb. 13:8, KJV:

   Jesus Christ the same yesterday, and to day, and for ever.

2. *The promise that thrilled you.*

I Kings 8:56, KJV:

Blessed be the Lord, that hath given rest unto his people Israel, according to all that he promised: there hath not failed one word of all his good promise, which he promised by the hand of Moses his servant.

3. *The power which will enable you to finish your course.*

Phil. 1:6, KJV:

...being confident of this very thing; that he which hath begun a good work in you will perform it until the day of Christ Jesus.

The primary Greek verb for "call" is *kaleo* (Strong's #2564) which means "to call (aloud)." It means to call or summon with a loud voice, an invitation. It is taken from the word *keleuo* (#2753) which means "to incite by word; order." The latter is rendered in the English Bible as "bid, command." This word is further reduced to the root *kello*, which means "to urge on."

We have heard the Voice of Jesus. It was a loud sound, a Feast of Trumpets that raised us from the death of trespasses and sins. He has "digged" our ears and given us faith to believe. Out of Egypt He has called His son.

The Voice of the One who called us now lives within us! There, in our spirit, undaunted and untouched by the circumstantial realm, the Voice of our Beloved is ever, always, urging us on! We have not quit because we cannot quit. Better said, we have died and our lives are hid with Christ in God. Our life has been replaced by the life of the One who did not quit, the One who endured unto the end. He died as us that we might live as Him.

The inward urgency of the Kingdom of God is the Voice of the King within His people.

This is not the bulldoggedness of Adam's efforts, the stubbornness of man which refuses to consider that it might be God and not the devil who is shutting down certain ministries in the land. This perseverance is not the fear of failure which drives men to give birth to one Ishmael after another because they have not heard from God; it is, rather, the faith of God, the faith that God has in Himself as He lives in and through His chosen priesthood.

In the 1990s, the called cannot quit or fail; all others will and must. The still, small Voice from within our hearts is ever, always, urging us on. This is not the soulish "You can make it," but rather the sound of the Spirit, "Jesus made it!" Prophets can disappoint you. The Son is ever faithful.

Ps. 138:8, KJV:

The Lord will perfect that which concerneth me: thy mercy, O Lord, endureth for ever: forsake not the works of thine own hands.

Ps. 138:8, NIV:

The Lord will fulfill his purpose for me; your love, O Lord, endures forever—do not abandon the works of your hands.

Phil. 1:6, NIV:

...being confident of this, that he who began a good work in you will carry it on to completion until the day of Christ Jesus.

Are you hurting? At a crossroads? Detoured by presumptuous prophecy? Then come to Jesus. Come now. Get the help you need. He is a Priest who can be touched.

Chapter 10

The Mountain Principle

A Priest Who Can Be Touched

The priesthood is changing. God's people are moving from the future to the present, from duality to simplicity, from two wills to one will, from the voices of the many to the Voice of the One. Now we find them moving from mountain to mountain, from Sinai to Zion. The priesthood from the throne of grace is accessible, transparent and secure.

Heb. 12:18-24, NIV:

You have not come to a mountain that can be touched and that is burning with fire; to darkness, gloom and storm;

to a trumpet blast or to such a voice speaking words, so that those who heard it begged that no further word be spoken to them,

because they could not bear what was commanded: "If even an animal touches the mountain, it must be stoned."

The sight was so terrifying that Moses said, "I am trembling with fear."

But you have come to Mount Zion, to the heavenly Jerusalem, the city of the living God. You have come to thousands upon thousands of angels in joyful assembly,

to the church of the firstborn, whose names are written in heaven. You have come to God, the judge of all men, to the spirits of righteous men made perfect,

to Jesus the mediator of a new covenant, and to the sprinkled blood that speaks a better word than the blood of Abel.

The Old Testament mountain says, "Keep away. No trespassing." The New Testament mountain says, "Whosoever will may come." The God of Sinai is the Lawgiver and appears to be angry and stern, the God of darkness, gloom and storm. The King in Zion is the revealer of grace and truth, the God of peace. He stepped from behind the curtain to reveal the Father of mercy and comfort.

The Old Testament saints were afraid of Yahweh, the God of Moses; in their minds, He could not be approached. To them, His commandments were unbearable. Their God was not cordial, could not be reached and was far away. Jesus came out from the bosom of the Father to declare the invisible God, the "happy" God (I Tim. 1:11). He wasted no time in letting men know that the Kingdom of Heaven was "at hand," that is, within their reach. For the first time, God could be touched.

1 John 1:1-3, NIV:

That which was from the beginning, which we have heard, which we have seen with our eyes, which we have looked at and our hands have touched—this we proclaim concerning the Word of life.

The life appeared; we have seen it and testify to it, and we proclaim to you the eternal life, which was with the Father and has appeared to us.

We proclaim to you what we have seen and heard, so that you also may have fellowship with us. And our fellowship is with the Father and with his Son, Jesus Christ.

Moses and the law had done a good job. By the law is the knowledge of sin (Rom. 3:20), and sin separates God and man. There was a great gulf, a partition, a wall, a veil that kept man out and kept God in. Moses emphasized the distance between God and His creation. Jesus came to remove the distance, to effect our reconciliation, taking hold of God with one hand and man with the other. He is our Propitiation, the Mercy-seat where God and man can once again meet in peace (Rom. 3:25).

Eph. 2:14-17, NIV:

For he himself is our peace, who has made the two one and has destroyed the barrier, the dividing wall of hostility,

by abolishing in his flesh the law with its commandments and regulations. His purpose was to create in himself one new man out of the two, thus making peace, and in this one body to reconcile both of them to God through the cross, by which he put to death their hostility.

He came and preached peace to you who were far away and peace to those who were near.

Jesus came to destroy every barrier, to break down every wall. Christians know all about walls; the American church is platform-oriented, expert at fellowshipping the back of somebody else's head. Too many of her preachers are slick, polished professionals, whisked behind the curtain at the final "amen." Jesus strode from behind the curtain that He might tear it into pieces, rend the veil, and once and for all remove the expanse between God and man. He rent the dividing wall of hostility from the top to the bottom. He filled the gulf with an unconditional love that requires no merit of performance. Jesus consecrated a new and living way for us into the Most Holy Place (Heb. 10:19-22). He is God Almighty in the flesh, the Incarnate Deity who still has time to hold babies and eat lunch with sinners. His is a priesthood which can be touched.

Heb. 4:14-16, NIV:

Therefore, since we have a great high priest who has gone through the heavens, Jesus the Son of God, let us hold firmly to the faith we profess.

For we do not have a high priest who is unable to sympathize with our weaknesses, but we have one who has been tempted in every way, just as we are—yet was without sin.

Let us then approach the throne of grace with con-
fidence, so that we may receive mercy and find grace to
help us in our time of need.

The Greek word for "touch" in Hebrews 4:15 is *sum-*
patheo (Strong's #4834), meaning "to feel sympathy with;
to commiserate." Webster defines "commiserate" as "to
feel or express compassion for." Consider the following
verses where this word and its related expressions are
used.

Heb. 10:34, NIV:

You sympathized with those in prison and joyfully
accepted the confiscation of your property, because you
knew that you yourselves had better and lasting posses-
sions.

1 Pet. 3:8, NIV:

Finally, all of you, live in harmony with one
another; be sympathetic, love as brothers, be compas-
sionate and humble.

Rom. 8:17, NIV:

Now if we are children, then we are heirs—heirs of
God and co-heirs with Christ, if indeed we share in his
sufferings in order that we may also share in his glory.

1 Cor. 12:26, NIV:

If one part suffers, every part suffers with it; if one
part is honored, every part rejoices with it.

These verses speak for themselves, asking every
leader a few simple questions. Does this describe your
local church at the present time? How close are you to

your people? How close are your people to each other? What is your accessibility rating? Take your own temperature.

God is changing the priesthood by removing the stony, callous heart of our apathy and indifference and replacing it with a heart of flesh, pulsing with sensitivity for others. He is dealing with the superficiality of our shallow relationships and our idolatry in still having a best-loved preacher, choosing whom we love and what we want to hear. All that is being consumed as we draw near to the Lord and to one another.

Ps. 133:1-3, NIV:

How good and pleasant it is when brothers live together in unity!

It is like precious oil poured on the head, running down on the beard, running down on Aaron's beard, down upon the collar of his robes.

It is as if the dew of Hermon were falling on Mount Zion. For there the Lord bestows his blessing, even life forevermore.

Our heavenly Aaron rent the veil, rose again, passed through the heavens, and was crowned with glory and honor (Heb. 2:9). The kingly oil of glad coronation cascaded over His head and now flows down upon His Body. The love which enabled Him to open His heart to planet earth has been poured out (Rom. 5:5), empowering us to open ourselves to Him and to all those for whom He died.

The City of Clean, Clear Glass

Not only is this new order of priesthood accessible; its members are transparent. There are no masks, no veneers, no facades, no put-ons, no phoneys. Just real people. Unlike the previous Feast with its religious leaven of hypocrisy and partiality, the Feast of Tabernacles is taking away the false face of Moses, bringing God's people into the experiential glory of the face of Jesus. These will be a people of light and understanding. Jesus knew that when He first called His Church a City.

Matt. 5:14, KJV:

> *Ye are the light of the world. A city that is set on an hill cannot be hid.*

Matt. 16:18, KJV:

> *And I say also unto thee, That thou art Peter, and upon this rock I will build my church; and the gates of hell shall not prevail against it.*

Heb. 11:10, KJV:

> *For he looked for a city which hath foundations, whose builder and maker is God.*

Heb. 12:22-23, KJV:

> *But ye are come unto mount Sion, and unto the city of the living God, the heavenly Jerusalem, and to an innumerable company of angels,*
>
> *To the general assembly and church of the firstborn, which are written in heaven, and to God the Judge of all, and to the spirits of just men made perfect...*

Rev. 21:9-10, KJV:

And there came unto me one of the seven angels which had the seven vials full of the seven last plagues, and talked with me, saying, Come hither, I will shew thee the bride, the Lamb's wife.

And he carried me away in the spirit to a great and high mountain, and shewed me that great city, the holy Jerusalem, descending out of heaven from God...

Ps. 48:1-2, NIV:

Great is the Lord, and most worthy of praise, in the city of our God, his holy mountain.

It is beautiful in its loftiness, the joy of the whole earth. Like the utmost heights of Zaphon is Mount Zion, the city of the Great King.

The Bride, the Lamb's Wife, is a City. This City is the heavenly Jerusalem, the Church. The hill, the great high mountain, is Zion. The Great King is Jesus. We are not marching to Zion; Zion is marching. We are not looking for a city; we are the City! This City is the people for which Abraham sought. This City is descending from the heavens to the earth, from the invisible to the visible, from the mystical to the practical, from the platform to the pew, from the building to the streets. In the 1990s, the Kingdom of God must be perceived, proclaimed and, above all, performed.

John saw the manifold splendor of this City. There is a rich study in my verse-by-verse treatment of Revelations 21, a booklet and tape series called *The Twelve Gates of the City.* The important point here is that the City was made of transparent glass.

Rev. 21:18, KJV:

And the building of the wall of it was of jasper: and the city was pure gold, like unto clear glass.

Rev. 21:21, KJV:

And the twelve gates were twelve pearls: every several gate was of one pearl: and the street of the city was pure gold, as it were transparent glass.

The Greek word for "transparent" here is *diaphanes* (Strong's #1307) and means "appearing through; diaphonous." Webster says that "diaphonous" means "allowing to shine or appear through, transparent, clear." *Diaphanes* is taken from two other words:

1. *dia* (#1223) = "the channel of an act; through" and

2. *phaino* (#5316) = "to lighten (shine); show."

Compare the noun *phos* (#5457), which means "luminousness" and is translated as "fire, light." Note the verb *phao*, which means "to shine or make manifest, especially by rays." The noun *phosphoros* (#5459) is given as "light-bearing, the morning star, day star." The companion verb *photizo* (#5461) means "to shed rays, to shine, to brighten up," and is translated as "enlighten, illumine, bring to light, give light, make to see."

Mal. 4:2, KJV:

But unto you that fear my name shall the Sun of righteousness arise with healing in his wings; and ye shall go forth, and grow up as calves of the stall.

Others further explain this verse: "...with healing in its beams" (*Berkeley*).

"...with healing in its rays" (*RSV*).

"...the saving Sun shall arise with healing in his rays" (*Moffatt*).

"...with healing upon his lips" (*Lamsa*).

John 8:12, KJV:

> *Then spake Jesus again unto them, saying, I am the light of the world: he that followeth me shall not walk in darkness, but shall have the light of life.*

Jesus is the Light. The Son is the Sun, the Bright Morning Star. It is the light of His life that is shining through the City, the Church. We are to give that light to others, causing them to see. Our walk (the street of the City) is in Him and after His divine nature (pure gold). When Peter got up one morning and walked down to the coffee shop, he was as surprised as anyone to see folks on both sides of the street being healed. His "shadow" (Acts 5:15) was the outraying effulgence of the Christ from within!

Once we understand that the word for "clear" in Revelation 21:18 means "clean," the picture gets brighter. Clean, clear glass. We have stepped across the threshhold of the Most Holy Place with the awareness and vision of a clean, clear Church. In the Holy Place, we saw through a glass darkly. The grubby little fingerprints of Adam smudged the view. The air was clouded by the flies in the ointment (Eccl. 10:1). But in the Most Holy Place, we mature and meet Him face to face. Moses' face was veiled and closed, especially in the reading of the Scriptures (II Cor. 3:13-15). Those who are determined to stop at the Feast of Pentecost have closed their heart and ears lest they hear anything beyond what they have been taught. But the face of Jesus in His people is unveiled and open, teachable, willing to change and grow.

Finally, to complete the picture, note that the word for "glass" in Revelation 21:18, 21 is *hualos* (#5194) and means "glass (as being transparent like rain)." It is related to *huetos* (#5205), "rain or shower." Compare this with the "sea of glass" in Revelation 4:6, 15:2. When the Church gets honest with God, the showers will come.

In the 1980s, the world watched and laughed as the Church was humiliated and embarrassed by her sins. When the 1990s began, God turned the corner. The scoffers and scorners are drying up and withering in a parched land (Ps. 68:6). At the same time, God is preparing clouds with water. As we become like Him, His light shines through us and His life is poured out like rain from us. The priesthood of the Most Holy Place will reign and rain on the earth (Rev. 5:10).

The City Without Walls

This priesthood is ever becoming more accessible and transparent. But what is the key to this kind of confidence? This City, this people, this priesthood is without walls, a powerful truth detailed in the fourth chapter of *The More Excellent Ministry*. This new breed of ministry is secure, knowing who they are in Christ.

Zech. 2:4-5, KJV:

And said unto him, Run, speak to this young man, saying, Jerusalem shall be inhabited as towns without walls for the multitude of men and cattle therein:

For I, saith the Lord, will be unto her a wall of fire round about, and will be the glory in the midst of her.

Walls are for protection; they keep people out. We all have them. These defense mechanisms vary from person to person. For example, some of us used to be adept at hiding behind the Scriptures; we were clever, not wise. Not wanting to change, we tuck ourselves away in seemingly safe comfort zones. But the Lord has issued a search and seizure warrant with our name on it. He stands at the door and knocks (Rev. 3:20), summoning us to share the ministry of the Most Holy Place, a priesthood that is open and vulnerable. How can we become that kind of people?

Col. 3:3, NIV:

For you died, and your life is now hidden with Christ in God.

2 Tim. 1:12, NIV:

That is why I am suffering as I am. Yet I am not ashamed, because I know whom I have believed, and am convinced that he is able to guard what I have entrusted to him for that day.

1 Pet. 1:5, NIV:

...who through faith are shielded by God's power until the coming of the salvation that is ready to be revealed in the last time.

I Pet. 1:5, KJV:

Who are kept by the power of God through faith unto salvation ready to be revealed in the last time.

The answer is simple: This ministry and people is secure in Christ. The cloud of God has led us through the wilderness of our adolescence; the Lord Himself has been our desert shield. Jesus, not the horse and rider, is our Ark of safety and preservation. There is a place of rest in Him that is only now being discovered. We know who we are in Christ and why He sent us. We no longer apologize for obeying His voice, having begun to tap into a measure of rest and liberty in Him that we had not experienced before. The Lord continues to bring His people to a daily, constant, complete dependency on Him for all things. We have learned how to curl up in the lap of our Father. There we are safe.

Rom. 14:17, KJV:

For the kingdom of God is not meat and drink; but righteousness, and peace, and joy in the Holy Ghost.

Righteousness is right relationship. Peace is security. Joy is expression. Where there is no expression, there is no security. Where there is no security, something about our relationship with God or man is not right. This unrighteousness is the religious imagery that portrays and projects a God who is distant, One who can only be followed afar off and who cannot be approached. According to tradition, this same God will, if we are good enough, let us come and live with Him one day, and will give us rest when we finally see Him face to face. This God, however, is the God of Sinai. This is not the God of Zion.

Jonah 2:8-9, KJV:

They that observe lying vanities forsake their own mercy.

But I will sacrifice unto thee with the voice of thanksgiving; I will pay that I have vowed. Salvation is of the Lord.

Jonah 2:8-9, NIV:

Those who cling to worthless idols forfeit the grace that could be theirs.

But I, with a song of thanksgiving, will sacrifice to you. What I have vowed I will make good. Salvation comes from the Lord.

The Feast of Pentecost is plagued by insecurity because of the duality we learned of in Chapter Seven. This in turn makes people and preachers try to perform and to live right. Our own efforts are miserable, futile attempts to fulfill the expectations of others. When we give place to this false imagery, we forsake our own mercy. May His love teach us that the only expectation that we must meet is His, and He expects us to be what we are . . . anointed. Everything that you or I have done, are doing, or will do doesn't count. Salvation is of the Lord.

Another problem with the performance syndrome is that everyone likes to grade his performance, not to mention the conduct of others. Paul called this "imputing their trespasses unto them" in Second Corinthians 5:19. Men who build their own kingdoms often require these "command performances." Human estimates, denominational standards, rules and regulations are not enough. The Man who did the measuring in the Books of Zechariah and Revelation is the same Man who measured Ezekiel's Temple, the Temple we are. He is the Man Christ Jesus.

Ezek. 40:1-5, NIV:

In the twenty-fifth year of our exile, at the beginning of the year, on the tenth of the month, in the fourteenth year after the fall of the city—on that very day the hand of the Lord was upon me and he took me there.

In visions of God he took me to the land of Israel and set me on a very high mountain, on whose south side were some buildings that looked like a city.

He took me there, and I saw a man whose appearance was like bronze; he was standing in the gateway with a linen cord and a measuring rod in his hand.

The man said to me, "Son of man, look with your eyes and hear with your ears and pay attention to everything I am going to show you, for that is why you have been brought here. Tell the house of Israel everything you see."

I saw a wall completely surrounding the temple area. The length of the measuring rod in the man's hand was six long cubits, each of which was a cubit and a handbreadth. He measured the wall; it was one measuring rod thick and one rod high.

The very high mountain is Zion. The linen cord is His righteous measure. His standard is six cubits and a span. Six is the number of man. His measure is a hand beyond what a man can do. Incidentally, we are now living in the "span" between two ages, between two priesthoods, between six and seven. Any measure other than His measure is an unrighteous measure.

2 Cor. 10:12, NIV:

> *We do not dare to classify or compare ourselves with some who commend themselves. When they measure themselves by themselves and compare themselves with themselves, they are not wise.*

The fire of the Most Holy Place is consuming our yardsticks. His life is the measure by which all men are judged, and no one can measure up to that. The only filler for the hole in the core of man is unconditional love, and the name of unconditional love is Jesus. No man deserves such love, cannot nor ever will earn such love, and cannot add to or take away from such love. Jesus Christ, the love of God, is perfect. Only He can satisfy and make us secure. Once the wall is down in our relationship with God, we can love and serve others as we should. Only a free man can set a man free. I must see the Christ in me, and me in Christ; then I can be a fruitful Christian.

Many Christians have been closed, hypocritical and insecure; we have miserably failed in the stewardship of God's gifts. I speak not of finance, but of people. On behalf of all the preachers, I ask the saints to forgive us. We did not know who we were in Him, and could not properly receive, assimilate and administrate the gifts of God: you His people. There have been casualties in the Kingdom because we failed to have a vision of our own worth in Christ. With such dim sight, how could we properly value the people who had been entrusted to our care? Because of our reluctance to receive from the Father (because of pride, the fear of failure), we have often taken the dealings of God, the commitments He requires of leaders, and projected to the saints a burden that they have not the grace to bear. Thank God that these are days of recovery! He is restoring the years (Joel 2:25). Only God can fathom the extent of His reconciling love, and only God can heal broken relationships. Many of us preachers now have the courage to face the One who stripped away some of those gifts so that we might become aware of their worth. The heart of the fathers is turning.

Mal. 4:5-6, KJV:

> Behold, I will send you Elijah the prophet before the coming of the great and dreadful day of the Lord:

> And he shall turn the heart of the fathers to the children, and the heart of the children to their fathers, lest I come and smite the earth with a curse.

This irresponsible stewardship goes both ways. Once the heart of the fathers is turned to the children, the heart of the children must be turned to the fathers. Every ministry is a gift from God, and many of the saints have not handled us in a godly manner. Some have reaped domestically their own previous rebellion and mockery of genuine spiritual authority. The saints must forgive and bless every ministry that ever touched their lives. The 1990s will feature the Church giving honor to whom honor is due. Many sons are going to return, especially in attitude, to the fathers. In this decade, there will be a definite change in posture toward ministry. It's time for all of us to make things right. The door is open and the table is spread. J. T. Cardwell, an elder here for many years, taught us that a relationship is like an egg. Many eggs have been dropped by shepherds and sheep alike. God is now offering each of us a new egg. The name of this new egg is hope. Finish reading this paragraph, and then go do what is right. Healing and restoration await you.

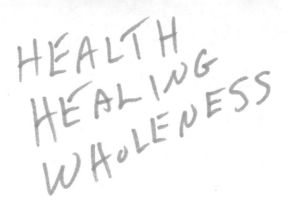

Chapter 11

The Man Principle

He Will Heal Us in the Third Day

The Priest in Zion is better than the priesthood of Sinai. As we continue to develop from the Feast of Pentecost to the Feast of Tabernacles, we mature from the blessing of healing to union with the Healer. This is termed the Man Principle because the whole man is to be healed. This completed work happens in the third day in the Most Holy Place.

Hos. 6:1-3, KJV:

> *Come, and let us return unto the Lord: for he hath torn, and he will heal us; he hath smitten, and he will bind us up.*

> *After two days will he revive us: in the third day he will raise us up, and we shall live in his sight.*

> *Then shall we know, if we follow on to know the Lord: his going forth is prepared as the morning; and he shall come unto us as the rain, as the latter and former rain unto the earth.*

Hos. 6:1-3, NIV:

Come, let us return to the Lord. He has torn us to pieces but he will heal us; he has injured us but he will bind up our wounds.

After two days he will revive us; on the third day he will restore us, that we may live in his presence.

Let us acknowledge the Lord; let us press on to acknowledge him. As surely as the sun rises, he will appear; he will come to us like the winter rains, like the spring rains that water the earth.

2 Pet. 3:8, NIV:

But do not forget this one thing, dear friends: With the Lord a day is like a thousand years, and a thousand years are like a day.

Two days represent two thousand years. The seventh day from Adam, the third day from Jesus, is upon us. The Feast of Passover was in the first month, the Feast of Pentecost in the third month, and the Feast of Booths in the seventh month (Lev. 23, Deut. 16). Reckoned from Adam, we are living in a transition time between the sixth and seventh days; the seventh day is to be paralleled with the seventh month, the time of the Feast of Tabernacles. Reckoned from Jesus, the second day is ending and the third day is beginning.

Isa. 43:18-21, NIV:

Forget the former things; do not dwell on the past.

See, I am doing a new thing! Now it springs up; do you not perceive it? I am making a way in the desert and streams in the wasteland.

The wild animals honor me, the jackals and the owls, because I provide water in the desert and streams in the wasteland, to give drink to my people, my chosen,

the people I formed for myself that they may proclaim my praise.

A new thing is being birthed as we stand on the brink of the seventh day from Adam and the third day from Jesus. The prophet Hosea declared that God would quicken His people after two days, and in the third day He would raise them up. Jesus walked this earth the day before yesterday, 2,000 years ago. It's time for Him to heal us.

John 2:18-22, KJV:

Then answered the Jews and said unto him, What sign shewest thou unto us, seeing that thou doest these things?

Jesus answered and said unto them, Destroy this temple, and in three days I will raise it up.

Then said the Jews, Forty and six years was this temple in building, and wilt thou rear it up in three days?

But he spake of the temple of his body.

When therefore he was risen from the dead, his disciples remembered that he had said this unto them; and they believed the scripture, and the word which Jesus had said.

I Cor. 3:16, KJV:

Know ye not that ye are the temple of God, and that the Spirit of God dwelleth in you?

Luke 13:31-32, KJV:

> *The same day there came certain of the Pharisees, saying unto him, Get thee out, and depart hence: for Herod will kill thee.*
>
> *And he said unto them, Go ye, and tell that fox, Behold, I cast out devils, and I do cures today and tomorrow, and the third day I shall be perfected.*

Luke 13:31-32, NIV:

> *At that time some Pharisees came to Jesus and said to him, "Leave this place and go somewhere else. Herod wants to kill you."*
>
> *He replied, "Go tell that fox, 'I will drive out demons and heal people today and tomorrow, and on the third day I will reach my goal.'"*

The Church is His Temple, His Body. Jesus has been casting out demons and healing sick bodies and minds for two thousand years. Now it is time for Him to have mercy upon Zion, to be perfected in a people, to complete His purpose in their spirits, to reach His goal. He's not perfecting us; He's perfecting Himself in us. The word for "perfected" in Luke 13:32 is *teleioo* (Strong's #5048) and means "to complete, accomplish, or consummate in character." It is translated "consecrate, finish, fulfill, perfect, make perfect," and is used 24 times in the New Testament, the Bible number of priesthood. Consider these examples.

John 4:34, KJV: *1 Cor 13:10*

> *Jesus saith unto them, My meat is to do the will of him that sent me, and to finish his work.*

John 17:22-23, NIV:

I have given them the glory that you gave me, that they may be one as we are one:

I in them and you in me. May they be brought to complete unity to let the world know that you sent me and have loved them even as you have loved me.

Heb. 2:10-11, NIV:

In bringing many sons to glory, it was fitting that God, for whom and through whom everything exists, should make the author of their salvation perfect through suffering.

Both the one who makes men holy and those who are made holy are of the same family. So Jesus is not ashamed to call them brothers.

I John 4:17-18, KJV:

Herein is our love made perfect, that we may have boldness in the day of judgment: because as he is, so are we in this world. ✦ 5046

There is no fear in love; but perfect love casteth out fear: because fear hath torment. He that feareth is not made perfect in love.

The word *teleioo* is taken from *teleios* (#5046), "complete." This in turn is from the root *telos* or *tello* (#5056) which means "to set out for a definite point or goal; the conclusion of an act or state; result; purpose." It is used 42 times in the New Testament. Compare the 42 generations of the first chapter of Matthew and remember that 42 is 6 x 7, or man brought to perfection . . . a perfect

Man, a mature Church. This one new Man is spoken of in the following passages where *teleios* is used.

Matt. 5:48, NIV:

> *Be perfect, therefore, as your heavenly Father is perfect.*

1 Cor. 13:8-13, NIV:

> *Love never fails. But where there are prophecies, they will cease; where there are tongues, they will be stilled; where there is knowledge, it will pass away.*

> *For we know in part and we prophesy in part,*

> *but when perfection comes, the imperfect disappears.*

> *When I was a child, I talked like a child, I thought like a child, I reasoned like a child. When I became a man, I put childish ways behind me.*

> *Now we see but a poor reflection; then we shall see face to face. Now I know in part; then I shall know fully, even as I am fully known.*

> *And now these three remain: faith, hope and love. But the greatest of these is love.*

Eph. 4:13, KJV:

> *...Till we all come in the unity of the faith, and of the knowledge of the Son of God, unto a perfect man, unto the measure of the stature of the fulness of Christ...*

Eph. 4:13, NIV:

...until we all reach unity in the faith and in the knowledge of the Son of God and become mature, attaining to the whole measure of the fullness of Christ.

All of this happens in the third day. Another entire book could be written on this subject as exampled below. God's people are going to hear more and more about this truth in the next few years. On the third day:

1. *The waters under the heaven were gathered together into one place and the earth yielded fruit (Gen. 1:9-13).*

2. *Abraham saw the mountain of sacrifice (Gen. 22:4).*

3. *The Lord came down in the sight of all the people (Ex. 19:11-16).*

4. *The remainder of the flesh of the sacrifice was burned with fire (Lev. 7:17-18).*

5. *The news of Saul's death was announced (II Sam. 1:2).*

6. *Hezekiah was healed and went up to the house of the Lord (II Kings 20:5-8).*

7. *The house of the Lord was finished (Ezra 6:15).*

8. *Esther put on her royal apparel and stood in the inner court, obtaining favor from the king and deliverance for her people (Esther 5:1-6).*

9. *There was a marriage feast in Cana of Galilee, water was turned to wine, and seven pots were filled (John 2:1).*

There is a time to heal (Eccl. 3:1-3). God has ordained the third day as His season to heal man completely (I Thess. 5:23). We are to be made whole—spirit, soul and body. The whole man is to be delivered and come into union with the Healer in the Most Holy Place in the third day.

Healing in the Old Testament

In the Outer Court, there is healing; in the Holy Place, there is health; in the Most Holy Place, there is life (John 14:6). To better understand this, look at the subject of healing. Webster defines "healing" as "tending to cure; remedial, curative; becoming sound, well or healthy again." He adds that "heal" means "to make whole; restore to health; to cure or get rid of a disease; to free from grief, troubles or evil; to make up a breach or differences; to reconcile." To be healed is to be whole!

Man is a trichotomy: spirit, soul, and body; *pneuma*, *psyche* and *soma*. The Greek word for "salvation" is *soteria* and means "a complete deliverance." The total subject of healing includes all three dimensions.

In the Old Testament, the word that is used more than any other for "healing" is *rapha* (Strong's #7495), "to mend by stitching; to cure." It is translated "cure, (cause to) heal, physician, repair, make whole." This word is common to both ancient and modern Hebrew, occurring approximately 65 times in the Hebrew Old Testament. Its first usage therein shows the power of evangelism and fruitfulness.

Gen. 20:17-18, NIV:

Then Abraham prayed to God, and God healed Abimelech, his wife and his slave girls so they could have children again,

for the Lord had closed up every womb in Abimelech's household because of Abraham's wife Sarah.

A large number of the uses of *rapha* express the healing of the nation, such healing not only involving God's grace and forgiveness, but also the nation's repentance. Also, the image of sickness is used in other passages to portray the ravages of sin. In these contexts, healing speaks of forgiveness and the restoration of a harmonious relationship with God, as well as the blessings that follow such a relationship (Isa. 1:4-6, 18-19; II Chron. 7:14; Hos. 6:1). The pronounced sound of the word *rapha* suggests a sewing machine; its significations are rich:

1. *Rapha signifies a sewing together. God desires to mend hearts, homes, churches or nations that have been rent by sin.*

2. *It signifies curing a wounded person, often done by sewing up the wound, as in Isaiah 19:22.*

3. *It signifies forgiveness, as in Hosea 14:4.*

4. *It signifies comforting the wounded, as in Job 13:4.*

5. *It signifies a rendering wholesome, as the curing of the bad water in Second Kings 2:21-22.*

In the third day, God is mending, curing, forgiving, and comforting His Church. The water of life is flowing freely. We are being healed. The word *rapha* is used in the following verses:

Ex. 15:26, KJV:

...And said, If thou wilt diligently hearken to the voice of the Lord thy God, and wilt do that which is right in his sight, and wilt give ear to his command- ments, and keep all his statutes, I will put none of these diseases upon thee, which I have brought upon the Egyptians: for I am the Lord that healeth thee.

Ps. 103:3, KJV:

...Who forgiveth all thine iniquities; who healeth all thy diseases...

Ps. 107:20, KJV:

He sent his word, and healed them, and delivered them from their destructions.

Isa. 53:5, KJV:

But he was wounded for our transgressions, he was bruised for our iniquities: the chastisement of our peace was upon him; and with his stripes we are healed.

The subject of healing is found throughout the Bible. Some examples of healing in the Old Testament include:

1. *The opening of Rachel's womb (Gen. 30:22).*

2. *Moses' leprosy (Ex. 4:6-7, 30).*

3. *Miriam's leprosy (Num. 12:10-15).*

4. *The scourge of serpents (Num. 21:6-9).*

5. *Elijah's raising of the widow's son (I Kings 17:17-24).*

6. *Elisha's raising of the Shunammite's child (II Kings 4:18-37).*

7. *Naaman's cure (II Kings 5:1-19).*

8. *Hezekiah's cure (Isa. 38:21).*

9. *Nebuchadnezzar's restoration (Dan. 4).*

Healing in the New Testament

Turning to the New Testament, the Bible has more to say about healing, especially in the four Gospels and the Book of Acts. There are two major Greek words for "healing" — *therapeuo* and *iaomai.*

The word *therapeuo* (Strong's #2323) means "to wait upon menially; to adore (God); to relieve (of disease)." It is rendered in the King James as "cure, heal, worship" and is taken from *therapon* (#2324), which means "a menial attendant or servant," and the base of *theros* (#2330), which means "heat or summer."

Vine's Dictionary of New Testament Words adds that *therapeuo* means "to care for the sick, to treat, cure, or heal," and gives the English "therapeutics." It is interesting that 40 of the 43 times this word is used occur in the Synoptic Gospels and the Book of Acts. Also, only in Luke 4:23 in the proverb, "Physician, heal thyself," and in Luke 8:43 (the woman with the issue of blood who could not "be healed of any") does *therapeuo* denote healing by ordinary medical means. In the rest of the passages, as exampled below, this word is used to describe the supernatural healings wrought by Jesus and His disciples.

Matt. 10:1, KJV:

And when he had called unto him his twelve dis-
ciples, he gave them power against unclean spirits, to
cast them out, and to heal all manner of sickness and all
manner of disease.

Matt. 10:8, KJV:

Heal the sick, cleanse the lepers, raise the dead, cast
out devils: freely ye have received, freely give.

The word *iaomai* (Strong's #2390) means "to cure." It
is translated in the King James as "heal, make whole." In
the *Septuagint* (LXX), the Greek Old Testament, *iaomai*
stands frequently for the Hebrew *rapha*. Consider these
usages:

Matt. 8:8, KJV:

The centurion answered and said, Lord, I am not
worthy that thou shouldest come under my roof: but
speak the word only, and my servant shall be healed.

Luke 4:18, KJV:

The Spirit of the Lord is upon me, because he hath
anointed me to preach the gospel to the poor; he hath
sent me to heal the brokenhearted, to preach deliverance
to the captives, and recovering of sight to the blind, to
set at liberty them that are bruised...

Luke 5:17, KJV:

And it came to pass on a certain day, as he was
teaching, that there were Pharisees and doctors of the
law sitting by, which were come out of every town of

Galilee, and Judaea, and Jerusalem: and the power of the Lord was present to heal them.

Acts 9:34, KJV:

And Peter said unto him, Aeneas, Jesus Christ maketh thee whole: arise, and make thy bed. And he arose immediately.

Acts 10:38, KJV:

How God anointed Jesus of Nazareth with the Holy Ghost and with power: who went about doing good, and healing all that were oppressed of the devil; for God was with him.

James 5:16, NIV:

Therefore confess your sins to each other and pray for each other so that you may be healed. The prayer of a righteous man is powerful and effective.

I Pet. 2:24, KJV:

Who his own self bare our sins in his own body on the tree, that we, being dead to sins, should live unto righteousness: by whose stripes ye were healed.

1 Pet. 2:24, NIV:

He himself bore our sins in his body on the tree, so that we might die to sins and live for righteousness; by his wounds you have been healed.

Jesus Christ was the incarnation of Jehovah-Rapha. God wants us to be healed. The following are some of the many examples of healing from the ministry of Jesus:

1. *The nobleman's son (John 4:46-54).*

2. *Peter's mother-in-law (Matt. 8:14-17, Mark 1:29-31, Luke 4:38-39).*

3. *The man with the withered hand (Matt. 12:9-13, Mark 3:1-5, Luke 6:6-11).*

4. *The centurion's servant (Matt. 8:5-13, Luke 7:1-10).*

5. *The woman with the issue of blood (Matt. 9:20-22, Mark 5:25-34, Luke 8:43-48).*

6. *The ten lepers (Luke 17:11-19).*

7. *The man born blind (John 9).*

8. *Malchus (Luke 22:49-51).*

9. *The raising of the widow's son (Luke 7:11-16); of Jairus' daughter (Matt. 9:18-26, Mark 5:22-43, Luke 8:41-56), and of Lazarus (John 11:1-46).*

This is a broad subject, and deserves more attention than is given here. For your further study, consider also these examples of healing in the New Testament:

1. *By the seventy (Luke 10:17-20).*

2. *By the other disciples (Mark 9:39; John 14:12).*

3. *By the apostles (Acts 3:6-16; 4:10, 30; 9:34-35; 16:18).*

4. *By Peter (Acts 5:15-16).*

5. *By Paul (Acts 16:18, 19:11-12, 28:8-9).*

6. *Aeneas (Acts 9:34).*

7. *Dorcas is raised (Acts 9:40).*

8. *The lame man (Acts 3:1-11).*

9. *The cripple (Acts 14:10).*

Bible Truths Concerning Healing

Christians believe in healing and practice it through faith and believing prayer. Healing is precious and is the children's bread, the inheritance of the saints. For two days, two thousand years, Jesus has been healing the minds and bodies of His people. Now the third day is dawning. He is going to heal man's spirit, soul and body as a new priesthood is brought into union with Him, armed with the awareness that the Healer is within.

Rom. 5:12, NIV:

Therefore, just as sin entered the world through one man, and death through sin, and in this way death came to all men, because all sinned...

Sickness and diseases are called a curse (Deut. 28:1-61). Sin and sickness came upon the human race because of Adam's disobedience. Jesus Christ redeemed us from the curse through His death, burial, and resurrection. He redeemed man from sin, sickness, poverty, and death. We have been delivered from the law of sin and death (sickness).

Gal. 3:13-14, KJV:

Christ hath redeemed us from the curse of the law, being made a curse for us: for it is written, Cursed is every one that hangeth on a tree:

That the blessing of Abraham might come on the Gentiles through Jesus Christ; that we might receive the promise of the Spirit through faith.

Rom. 8:1-6, NIV:

Therefore, there is now no condemnation for those who are in Christ Jesus,

because through Christ Jesus the law of the Spirit of life set me free from the law of sin and death.

For what the law was powerless to do in that it was weakened by the sinful nature, God did by sending his own Son in the likeness of sinful man to be a sin offering. And so he condemned sin in sinful man,

in order that the righteous requirements of the law might be fully met in us, who do not live according to the sinful nature but according to the Spirit.

Those who live according to the sinful nature have their minds set on what that nature desires; but those who live in accordance with the Spirit have their minds set on what the Spirit desires.

The mind of sinful man is death, but the mind controlled by the Spirit is life and peace...

There are three different sources of healing. First, there is natural healing (Prov. 17:22). The human body itself has a healing ministry. Secondly, there is medical healing (Matt. 9:12). Throughout history, there have been physicians such as Dr. Luke who have ministered to the physical needs of people. There is nothing wrong with doctors and medicine. All wisdom is from God. Thirdly, there is Divine healing (Ps. 103:1-4). God can overrule both nature and man to bring forth healing. The source of Divine healing is the cross of Jesus Christ (Isa. 53). Jesus took not only our sins, but also our sicknesses in

His body. The Tree of Life was placed on the tree of death, that we might be made whole.

Matt. 8:16-17, KJV:

When the even was come, they brought unto him many that were possessed with devils: and he cast out the spirits with his word, and healed all that were sick:

That it might be fulfilled which was spoken by Esaias the prophet, saying, Himself took our infirmities, and bare our sicknesses.

Matt. 8:16-17, NIV:

When evening came, many who were demon-possessed were brought to him, and he drove out the spirits with a word and healed all the sick.

This was to fulfill what was spoken through the prophet Isaiah: "He took up our infirmities and carried our diseases."

Isa. 53:4-6, KJV:

Surely he hath borne our griefs, and carried our sorrows: yet we did esteem him stricken, smitten of God, and afflicted.

But he was wounded for our transgressions, he was bruised for our iniquities: the chastisement of our peace was upon him; and with his stripes we are healed.

All we like sheep have gone astray; we have turned every one to his own way; and the Lord hath laid on him the iniquity of us all.

Isa. 53:4-6, NIV:

Surely he took up our infirmities and carried our sorrows, yet we considered him stricken by God, smitten by him, and afflicted.

But he was pierced for our transgressions, he was crushed for our iniquities; the punishment that brought us peace was upon him, and by his wounds we are healed.

We all, like sheep, have gone astray, each of us has turned to his own way; and the Lord has laid on him the iniquity of us all.

These are key passages. Much more could be said (see my verse-by-verse notes on Isaiah 53). Jesus died for all men; He is the Surety of the New Covenant which He established by His death and resurrection. His suffering was the penalty due and the remedy by which man is to be restored. He was wounded ("tormented"—margin) for us. Healing for the spirit, mind and body of man is provided for in His atonement. Healing is the children's bread (Mark 7:24-30, Psa. 103:3).

However, there may be certain hindrances to our receiving these covenantal benefits of healing: sin (Isa. 59:2, Matt. 13:15); unbelief (Mark 6:5, Matt. 13:58); an unforgiving spirit (Matt. 5:23-24, 6:14-15); the abuse of our bodies (I Cor. 3:16-17, Phil. 2:25-30); not discerning the Lord's Body at His table (I Cor. 11:29-33); satanic resistance (Dan. 10:12-13), or a strained husband-wife relationship (I Pet. 3:1-7).

Finally, we mention several ways to receive healing. Keep in mind that the greater dimension of Tabernacles

will swallow up the lesser realm of Pentecost. We are not doing away with the practice of the basic things listed below, but are adding to our faith the greater glory of the Most Holy Place, knowing that God is going to heal the whole man in the third day. We have laid the foundation and gotten our building permit (Heb. 6:1-3); now let us go on to know the Lord and finish the building.

There are many questions to be answered concerning healing; it is not a cut-and-dried subject. The Bible teaches that a person can receive healing in many ways:

1. *By faith in Jesus Christ (Heb. 11:6, Matt. 6:5).*

2. *By the prayer of faith and anointing with oil (James 5:14).*

3. *By the laying on of believers' hands (Mark 16:17).*

4. *By prayer cloths (Acts 19:12).*

5. *By speaking and sending the Word (Ps. 107:20, Matt. 8:8).*

6. *By the gifts of the Holy Spirit (I Cor. 12:8-10).*

7. *By the Lord's Table (I Cor. 11:23-30).*

The Healing of the Nations

We have but scratched the surface of this glorious truth. Many times healing remains a mystery to me, for I have seen God miraculously heal unsaved people of the worst of diseases; and, after prayer and fasting by concerned loved ones and friends, I have watched in horror as deeply devoted Christians have died painful deaths. But this I know: God is the Healer! He has torn and He will heal us! Ultimately, Jehovah-Rapha will heal the nations, renovate

the heavens and the earth, and fill the universe with His life and health. The fourth chapter of Daniel shows the same panorama of redemption: like mankind, Nebuchadnezzar was humiliated and then restored.

Rom. 8:19-23, KJV:

> *For the earnest expectation of the creature waiteth for the manifestation of the sons of God.*
>
> *For the creature was made subject to vanity, not willingly, but by reason of him who hath subjected the same in hope,*
>
> *Because the creature itself also shall be delivered from the bondage of corruption into the glorious liberty of the children of God.*
>
> *For we know that the whole creation groaneth and travaileth in pain together until now.*
>
> *And not only they, but ourselves also, which have the firstfruits of the Spirit, even we ourselves groan within ourselves, waiting for the adoption, to wit, the redemption of our body.*

Rom. 8:19-23, NIV:

> *The creation waits in eager expectation for the sons of God to be revealed.*
>
> *For the creation was subjected to frustration, not by its own choice, but by the will of the one who subjected it, in hope*
>
> *that the creation itself will be liberated from its bondage to decay and brought into the glorious freedom of the children of God.*

We know that the whole creation has been groaning as in the pains of childbirth right up to the present time.

Not only so, but we ourselves, who have the firstfruits of the Spirit, groan inwardly as we wait eagerly for our adoption as sons, the redemption of our bodies.

Ezek. 47:12, KJV:

And by the river upon the bank thereof, on this side and on that side, shall grow all trees for meat, whose leaf shall not fade, neither shall the fruit thereof be consumed: it shall bring forth new fruit according to his months, because their waters they issued out of the sanctuary: and the fruit thereof shall be for meat, and the leaf thereof for medicine.

Rev. 22:1-2, KJV:

And he shewed me a pure river of water of life, clear as crystal, proceeding out of the throne of God and of the Lamb.

In the midst of the street of it, and on either side of the river, was there the tree of life, which bare twelve manner of fruits, and yielded her fruit every month: and the leaves of the tree were for the healing of the nations.

God's healing program is greater than the laying on of hands. It is ultimately found in the Most Holy Place as we understand and acknowledge that the Healer lives within (Job 6:13). We must learn how to release the Christ (Song 4:12-16, John 7:37-39). Don't seek healing; seek Him! The highest order of anything is to become it. The redemptive Name of God, Jehovah-Rapha, was fulfilled in Jesus Christ our Healer; so His Name or nature is being reproduced in the Church. We are ministering His healing, and are to become healing to others in His Name (I Cor. 6:17, I John 4:17). God has begun to heal the nations! The Feast of Tabernacles is a harvest feast that is beginning to realize an unprecedented reaping of the peoples of the earth.

Micah 4:1-2, KJV:

But in the last days it shall come to pass, that the mountain of the house of the Lord shall be established in the top of the mountains, and it shall be exalted above the hills; and people shall flow unto it.

And many nations shall come, and say, Come, and let us go up to the mountain of the Lord, and to the house of the God of Jacob; and he will teach us of his ways, and we will walk in his paths: for the law shall go forth of Zion, and the word of the Lord from Jerusalem.

Zech. 14:16, NIV:

Then the survivors from all the nations that have attacked Jerusalem will go up year after year to worship the King, the Lord Almighty, and to celebrate the Feast of Tabernacles.

Chapter 12

The Motive Principle

Seeking God's Hand or Seeking God's Face?

The order, the administration, is changing. God is dealing with us differently. My desire throughout this treatise has been to pinpoint and clarify the practical workings of this change. Before we examine the final two areas which bear upon our daily lives more than any other, namely, finance and government, it is important for us to pause and check our motives. What are we after? His hand or His face? Men get caught up in revelation knowledge and present truth (II Pet. 1:12) and then begin to practice idolatry in its strangest form: they worship at the altar of who they are becoming in Christ and forget the One who brought them out that He might bring them in.

To seek God's hand is to covenant with God for what He can do . . . His presents. To seek God's face is to covenant with God for who He is . . . His Presence. In the first chapter of my book *Prevail*, Jesus is presented as both Priest and King. Those thoughts are nine years old, but they still speak:

> *Until the Church gets right, what can we offer the world? If we proclaim the Gospel to the world with the same countenance that the world already wears, what good is it? We must speak a living word to a crippled humanity . . . That is what the world needs to hear. But the majority of the people of God are not happy. Why? Because they are feeding upon a message that is man-centered and not God-centered. They only know Jesus in one dimension. There are many facets to the wonder of His Person.*
>
> *Learn this basic principle: Jesus is a Priest and a King. The majority of the Church world is only interested in His being a Priest or the Merciful One who meets the needs of man. But the blessed emphasis of the Word of God is His Lordship. He is to be King and Ruler and Governor over my life and yours. Surely He will meet your needs, but He will also demand your obedience.*
>
> *Everywhere we turn today, we hear a man-centered Gospel. Greedy ministry appealing to greedy people. The carnal mind craves comfort and loves money. The program of God does not center in man, but is of, through, and to Him (Rom. 11:36)! The natural man is a fighter and a taker. The Mind of Christ is a Lover and a Giver. The carnal mind is centered in self-rule. The spiritual mind is centered in God-rule. Jesus is a Priest. Jesus is a King. We must learn about both dimensions of His ministry. We cannot project a loving Priest without the firm discipline of His Kingdom. And we*

cannot preach the Gospel of the Kingdom with mercy and compassion of His priesthood.

Why are you serving God? Most folks serve Him because of His gifts. They love the gift more than the Giver. They love His presents more than they love His Presence. Everybody will quickly say, "I love the Lord!" But why do you love the Lord? Many will answer, "I love Jesus because He saved me. He healed me. He baptized me with the Holy Ghost. He blessed me financially." That's not enough. If that is why you love Him, you desire gifts but not the Giver. If that is your frame of mind, you don't love the Lord (who is the King), you love the Priest.

There is a "greenhouse" way of thinking in our country that has been preached, prophesied, and ministered to the Body of Christ. Don't peddle that to our bloodbrothers who are suffering and dying for the cause of Christ in other lands. Some have foolishly tried, but they won't hear you. They cannot relate to a message of those who say, "You will never have to suffer. You will never have to hurt. You will never have to sacrifice. Just come to Jesus, and everything will be all right. So long as you are born again, He will come any minute to rapture you out of all your troubles and pressures." Men and women who take the Kingdom of God seriously cannot receive those lies. Following Jesus Christ will cost you your life (Matt. 16:24-26, 19:21-22; Luke 9:23, 14:26)!

I don't want to upset you, but there are many who love God for one reason: what He has done for them. That is a good reason. We all started there. Jesus is our Merciful Savior. He is Priest. But if we stop there, if we *bog down and stagnate at that starting point, if we build doctrinal and sectarian walls around those foundational truths, we will cut off God's moving in our lives. Our people will be imprisoned and bound by our own unbelief.*

Prevail, pp. 11-27

May God challenge the heart of every leader in the Body of Christ to take another look at his motive, his vision, and the kind of mind he is imparting to his hearers. I have counseled with too many frustrated pastors. They have reproduced a restless spirit in the people. They have stopped growing. Organizational limitations have bound their hands and they cannot embrace this new day (Luke 2:28). We must know Jesus as Priest and King. We must instill that balance in the lives of the people we lead. We must teach them by example and precept to love His Presence more than His presents.

Matt. 6:33, KJV:

But seek ye first the kingdom of God, and his righteousness; and all these things shall be added unto you.

Seeking His Hand in the Realm of the Body

These excesses and abuses are very evident in two ways. Men seek God's hand in the realm of the body as well as the realm of the soul. Both of these are to be contrasted with our seeking His face in the realm of the spirit.

The realm of the body is the natural realm. In the third chapter of *The More Excellent Ministry*, we learned the meaning of going "from faith to faith" (Rom. 1:17). We have moved out of elementary faith into the faith of God, having learned that the foundational faith of Hebrews 6:1-2 ("faith upon God") was faith for:

1. *Regeneration (a new heart through a new birth) and justification (a new standing with God).*

2. *The circumcision of the heart in water baptism by immersion in the Name of the Lord Jesus Christ.*

3. *The pentecostal experience of the Holy Ghost baptism with the initial evidence of speakng with other tongues.*

4. *The healing of our physical bodies.*

5. *The meeting of our personal financial needs.*

Jesus saved me, circumcised my heart, filled me with the Holy Ghost, healed my body and paid my bills. All of that is wonderful and true, and each of us must experience these basic truths for ourselves. But real faith, His faith, goes beyond that. Those five blessings are what He has done, gifts given from His hand. To relate to God only on those terms is to seek His works, what He can do for us and others.

The expression "power evangelism" is good terminology, for it certainly describes the supernatural ministry of Jesus. Everyone needs to see his preaching or teaching confirmed with signs following. Jesus did it, then He taught it (Acts 1:1). But we also are to become the sign and the wonder (Isa. 8:18). Announce a healing meeting that demonstrates the gifts of the Holy Ghost, and a crowd will come. Tell those same people that a Holy Ghost-filled teacher is coming to show how to walk in responsible, covenant love with God and His people, and a few show up. Ask any seasoned leader in the third world. The crying need today is not just for evangelists. They want teachers!

What about those who seek God's hand only for financial prosperity? The extremes of the "health and wealth" message have already produced enough bad fruit in this generation. Even more incredible is the continued practice of some of these con men who daily embarrass the ministry and the cause of Christ with their blatant merchandising of the Gospel. Still more appalling is the ignorance of God's people who are ever naive to such swindling.

Jer. 5:30-31, NIV:

A horrible and shocking thing has happened in the land:

The prophets prophesy lies, the priests rule by their own authority, and my people love it this way. But what will you do in the end?

2 Cor. 2:17, NIV:

Unlike so many, we do not peddle the word of God for profit. On the contrary, in Christ we speak before God with sincerity, like men sent from God.

What is your motive? Is it outreach without upreach? Is it power without purity? Is it to see sick bodies healed, while sick minds are still full of vain imaginations and sick spirits are still filthy? Is it to boast of having natural wealth and abundance while the inner man remains a pauper?

The last 40 years have seen these excesses. The "in-part" realm of the Feast of Pentecost has produced a mixed bag. That is why the Lord must change the priesthood. In the holiest of all, we will see Him face to face.

Seeking His Hand in the Realm of the Soul

Men have sought the works of God in the dimension of the body. We are grateful for all that He does in that realm, but this cannot be our motive for going on with Him. The numbers game, the statistics of those who get saved, or filled, or healed; the size of the congregation, or the building, or the budget . . . these are not our major concerns.

Even more subtle is the seeking of God's hand in the realm of the soul or mind. This was briefly mentioned in Chapter Nine as we were cautioned against being gathered unto knowledge. We are not being gathered unto a message, but unto Him who is Truth. The decade of the 1990s will see a tidal wave of revelation knowledge coming to the mainstream of the Spirit-filled Church. This fresh Word will completely consume the traditions of the elders. What men have despised and termed heretical will have become welcomed and refreshing truth in the next three to five years. By the end of the decade, the false hope of an any-minute rapture, certainly one of the biggest obstacles standing in the way of responsible spiritual growth, will have been long forgotten by those who love the Bible. God's people will have grown by leaps and bounds.

Dan. 12:3-4, KJV:

And they that be wise shall shine as the brightness of the firmament; and they that turn many to righteousness as the stars for ever and ever.

But thou, O Daniel, shut up the words, and seal the book, even to the time of the end: many shall run to and fro, and knowledge shall be increased.

Dan. 12:8-10, KJV:

And I heard, but I understood not: then said I, O my Lord, what shall be the end of these things?

And he said, Go thy way, Daniel: for the words are closed up and sealed till the time of the end.

Many shall be purified, and made white, and tried; but the wicked shall do wickedly: and none of the wicked shall understand; but the wise shall understand.

Knowledge shall be increased, both natural knowledge and spiritual knowledge, not to mention the ways and means of recording, reproducing and communicating that knowledge. About 100 hours went into writing this volume; my 386 computer and some good Bible software helped. Have you learned anything from this book? How much have you learned? How quickly did you learn it?

What took God twenty-five years to teach some of us will be imparted to you in ten. You are learning from our mistakes. Be wise and understand. As you grow, please stop and assess your motives. Why do want to know what God is saying to apostles and prophets? Knowledge is power. To what purpose is your becoming powerful?

Phil. 2:12-13, NIV:

Therefore, my dear friends, as you have always obeyed—not only in my presence, but now much more in my absence—continue to work out your salvation with fear and trembling,

for it is God who works in you to will and to act according to his good purpose.

Jesus has healed our bodies. He has begun to heal our minds. Only He by the power of His Word can transform the soul. Certainly the Lord is doing a work in us. But many, especially those in leadership, have been obsessed with their own development in the Lord. Their offices are filled with unopened tapes and unread books. Everyone wants to be on the "cutting edge," but few are cutting anything.

The Outer Court is the realm of the external; the Holy Place, the Feast of Pentecost, emphasizes the internal; the Most Holy Place, the Feast of Tabernacles, is the realm of nature, or being. External, internal, being . . . seeking God's hand in the body, seeking God's hand in the soul, seeking God's face in the spirit. Do you understand? What is our motive, our purpose, as we walk into the coming years? Our supreme passion must not be our own change. Our supreme passion must be Jesus, the One who is changing us. Him, not what He can do.

1 Cor. 3:5-7, NIV:

What, after all, is Apollos? And what is Paul? Only servants, through whom you came to believe—as the Lord has assigned to each his task.

I planted the seed, Apollos watered it, but God made it grow.

So neither he who plants nor he who waters is anything, but only God, who makes things grow.

John 12:32, KJV:

And I, if I be lifted up from the earth, will draw all men unto me.

Leaders, stop trying to change people. None of us is the Holy Ghost. Only the Lord can minister to the heart. Instead, we must preach the Word. All we can do is plant or water; God will give the increase. Proclaim Jesus. Lift up Jesus. Get them to Jesus. He will do the rest.

Thanksgiving, Praise, and Worship

In the Outer Court, we are thankful for gifts given by His hand. In the Holy Place, we praise the Lord, telling one another of the greatness of His hand. In the Most Holy Place, we worship and adore His face, His Person.

Most Spirit-filled people have never experienced real corporate worship. We are a thankful people who appreciate what God has given. Most of us are acquainted with the Tabernacle of David and the way to praise Him with our voices, our hands and our whole bodies. Incidentally, for those who think that God is nervous about all this noise and fanfare, pomp and pageantry, both sacramental and spontaneous, stick around. Some of us who are dangerously filled with the Holy Ghost are going to get "more vile" than this (II Sam. 6:22). But praise isn't music. It isn't singing choruses. God comes to church to hear His children singing out of the heart to their Father by the Spirit. We meet the Son in the C ..er Court, the Spirit in the Holy Place, and the Father beyond the rent veil. That could be another chapter: worshiping the Father.

John 4:21-24, KJV:

> *Jesus saith unto her, Woman, believe me, the hour cometh, when ye shall neither in this mountain, nor yet at Jerusalem, worship the Father.*

> *Ye worship ye know not what: we know what we worship: for salvation is of the Jews.*

> *But the hour cometh, and now is, when the true worshippers shall worship the Father in spirit and in truth: for the Father seeketh such to worship him.*

> *God is a Spirit: and they that worship him must worship him in spirit and in truth.*

The reason the Church in this nation has majored on thanksgiving and praise is that we have emphasized God's hand. We have rarely known worship because we have not sought His face.

One more thought: real praise and worship involves spiritual warfare, and all must be done from the posture of the finished work of Jesus Christ. This, too, would require another chapter (or another book). Praise and worship is the celebration of the Lord Jesus Himself and then of His eternal, once and for all, complete victory over all enemies. Our devotion is also the declaration to those whom He has vanquished that the warfare is accomplished. It is finished. Every knee must bow. Our focus is not His victory. All eyes are on the Champion

Himself. We look at David, not the headless giant beneath his feet.

Phil. 2:9-11, NIV:

Therefore God exalted him to the highest place and gave him the name that is above every name,

that at the name of Jesus every knee should bow, in heaven and on earth and under the earth,

and every tongue confess that Jesus Christ is Lord, to the glory of God the Father.

Eph. 3:10, NIV:

His intent was that now, through the church, the manifold wisdom of God should be made known to the rulers and authorities in the heavenly realms...

II Cor. 4:6-7, KJV:

For God, who commanded the light to shine out of darkness, hath shined in our hearts, to give the light of the knowledge of the glory of God in the face of Jesus Christ.

But we have this treasure in earthen vessels, that the excellency of the power may be of God, and not of us.

The priesthood is changing. We have moved from Joshua to Ephesians. We are standing with both feet on solid resurrection ground. We are not taking the land. Jesus already did that. We are now standing with Him, clothed in His armor, warding off anyone or anything that says otherwise. Jesus took the land. He had to. He was the Victor. He had to do what He was. The Victor had to win the victory. He's not our soon-coming King;

that's a cop-out. He is already King of kings and Lord of lords! Our Champion was, is and always will be totally victorious. His hand won the battle, but His face is the place of glory and triumph. Our celebration and declaration is about Him, not what He did. We lift up the Giver who has given that we might receive.

Chapter 13

The Money Principle

Taking Tithes and Receiving Tithes

We have examined our motives; now let us turn to the most practical subject of the nine: the Money Principle, the principle of biblical economics. A good spiritual thermometer is a man's attitude toward his finances. How does this fit into the scheme of a changing priesthood? Like everything else, tithing is in three dimensions and, as with other principles we have examined, it is revealed in the triad of body, soul and spirit. Before we examine these, let us consider our root text for this chapter.

Heb. 7:4-10, KJV:

Now consider how great this man [Melchisedec] *was, unto whom even the patriarch Abraham gave the tenth of the spoils.*

And verily they that are of the sons of Levi, who receive the office of the priesthood, have a commandment to take tithes of the people according to the law, that is, of their brethren, though they come out of the loins of Abraham:

But he whose descent is not counted from them received tithes of Abraham, and blessed him that had the promises.

And without all contradiction the less is blessed of the better.

And here men that die receive tithes; but there he receiveth them, of whom it is witnessed that he liveth.

And as I may so say, Levi also, who receiveth tithes, payed tithes in Abraham.

For he was yet in the loins of his father, when Melchisedec met him.

Gen. 14:18-20, NIV:

Then Melchizedek king of Salem brought out bread and wine. He was priest of God Most High,

and he blessed Abram, saying, "Blessed be Abram by God Most High, Creator of heaven and earth.

And blessed be God Most High, who delivered your enemies into your hand." Then Abram gave him a tenth of everything.

In the Feast of Pentecost, the tithe is taken. In the Feast of Tabernacles, the tithe is received. The priesthood after the order of Aaron takes finances by commandment. The priesthood after the order of Melchisedec receives finances by a higher law.

Because this is such a broad and important subject, we will first review what the Bible has to say about stewardship and the principle of liberality. Then we can better grasp the relevance of tithing in three dimensions.

The Nature of Stewardship

Stewardship is the practice of systematic and proportionate giving of time, abilities, and material possessions based on the conviction that these are a trust from God to be used in His service for the benefit of His Kingdom. It is a divine-human partnership, with God as the senior Partner. It is a way of life: the recognition of God's ownership of one's person, powers and possessions, and the faithful use of these for the advancement of His Kingdom in the earth.

The Lord Jesus Christ is the legal covenantal Owner of our time, talent and treasure. God is the Owner of all things (Gen. 14:19, 22; Ps. 24:1, 50:1-12, 68:19; 89:11, Hag. 2:8). Man is His steward, responsible and accountable to Him (Matt. 25:14-30, Luke 19:11-26). God is the Giver, the Possessor, the Owner and the Rewarder. Man is the receiver, the steward who may use, abuse or lose the possession. To show this, we note these owner-steward relationships:

1. *Life—what you have received (Gen. 1:27-28, Acts 17:25, James 1:17).*

2. *Time—what you have been allotted (Prov. 24:30-34, Ps. 90:12).*

3. *Talents—what you have been given to use (Matt. 25:14-30).*

4. *Possessions—what has been entrusted to you (Matt. 6:19-21, Col. 3:1-2).*

5. Finances—what you have labored for (I Cor. 16:1-2).

I Cor. 4:1-2, KJV:

Let a man so account of us, as of the ministers of Christ, and stewards of the mysteries of God.

Moreover it is required in stewards, that a man be found faithful.

1 Cor. 4:1-2, NIV:

So then, men ought to regard us as servants of Christ and as those entrusted with the secret things of God.

Now it is required that those who have been given a trust must prove faithful.

The steward in Bible days was usually an old, faithful slave. Consider Eliezer, the steward of Abraham (Gen. 15:2). He had been delegated the responsibility for his master's possessions and was the ruler of the household, a man of great authority (Gen. 24). Compare Erastus, named in Romans 16:23 as a chamberlain or steward. According to the rabbis, Moses was God's steward. We are stewards of God. In our covenant walk with the Lord, He has access to all that we have in the natural and we have access to all that He has in the supernatural. Nothing is ours. All belongs to him, and He can require it any time He wants to.

Josh. 7:20-21, KJV:

And Achan answered Joshua, and said, Indeed I have sinned against the Lord God of Israel, and thus and thus have I done:

When I saw among the spoils a goodly Babylonish garment, and two hundred shekels of silver, and a wedge of gold of fifty shekels weight, then I coveted them, and took them; and, behold, they are hid in the earth in the midst of my tent, and the silver under it.

Don't touch what belongs to God. The story of Achan in the seventh chapter of Joshua teaches a powerful principle: when we take what belongs to God (for example, the tithe), it becomes a curse to us. Achan allowed the lust of the eyes, the craving for material things, to come between him and his God. A "wedge" of gold had pierced and divided his affections. This impulse eventually cost him his finances and his family. Like the tithe, Jericho belonged to God. Jehovah had put a ban on the city (Josh. 6:18-19); it was to be devoted to the Lord as a burnt offering, and was used as one of the lessons to be learned in the new land. The "accursed thing" in Hebrew means literally the "devoted thing." If anyone touched what was to be offered to God, it would become "the accursed thing" to him. A priesthood carrying the Ark has crossed the river and is walking into new territory. The Jordan, the veil, is rent, and we are advancing into the Most Holy Place. There, and all along our journey from Egypt to Canaan, the tithe belongs to Jesus.

It's a new day. God trusts us! But there is an identity crisis in the Body of Christ. People do not know who they are in Him, so they do not know what they have in Him. The Gospel is good news, not bad news. The Lamb has been slain and His blood has washed away the sin of the world. The New Covenant is the revelation that we have been reconciled to God and that we can be forgiven and saved. God is for us and not against us (Rom. 8:31). God has faith in Himself, and He sees Himself in His Church. So put away the spirit of fear and step out in your giving, knowing that a faithful God will meet you and not allow you to fall. This is the very basis of His building His government into us: He is a God who can be trusted.

The Principle of Liberality

II Cor. 8:1-2, KJV:

Moreover, brethren, we do you to wit of the grace of God bestowed on the churches of Macedonia;

How that in a great trial of affliction the abundance of their joy and their deep poverty abounded unto the riches of their liberality.

2 Cor. 8:1-5, NIV:

And now, brothers, we want you to know about the grace that God has given the Macedonian churches.

Out of the most severe trial, their overflowing joy and their extreme poverty welled up in rich generosity.

For I testify that they gave as much as they were able, and even beyond their ability. Entirely on their own,

they urgently pleaded with us for the privilege of sharing in this service to the saints.

And they did not do as we expected, but they gave themselves first to the Lord and then to us in keeping with God's will.

Paul taught more about giving in Second Corinthians chapters eight and nine than in any other of his writings. He used the church at Philippi (Acts 16) as an example of liberality. A legal giver gives because he has to. A loving giver gives because he wants to. A loving giver is a godly giver; he gives like God gives. This little band of Christians, the first church established in Europe, was like that. They put the megachurch at Corinth to shame.

The Bible says that money is not evil in itself; money is neither moral nor amoral, but neutral. There is no bad money on the planet, just bad people. The love of money is the root of all evil, and a man doesn't have to have any to love it (I Tim. 6:10). Have you ever wondered why there is such a popular clamor for golden streets and pearly gates? These kinds of things mean nothing to the spiritual man who understands that the trying of his faith is more precious than gold that perishes. Besides, how could corruptible gold have anything to do with an incorruptible inheritance? Selah.

I Pet. 1:3-7, KJV:

> *Blessed be the God and Father of our Lord Jesus Christ, which according to his abundant mercy hath begotten us again unto a lively hope by the resurrection of Jesus Christ from the dead,*
>
> *To an inheritance incorruptible, and undefiled, and that fadeth not away, reserved in heaven for you,*
>
> *Who are kept by the power of God through faith unto salvation ready to be revealed in the last time.*
>
> *Wherein ye greatly rejoice, though now for a season, if need be, ye are in heaviness through manifold temptations:*

*That the trial of your faith, being much more pre-
cious than of gold that perisheth, though it be tried with
fire, might be found unto praise and honour and glory
at the appearing of Jesus Christ...*

I Pet. 1:18-19, KJV:

*Forasmuch as ye know that ye were not redeemed
with corruptible things, as silver and gold, from your
vain conversation received by tradition from your
fathers;*

*But with the precious blood of Christ, as of a lamb
without blemish and without spot...*

1 Pet. 1:18-19, NIV:

*For you know that it was not with perishable things
such as silver or gold that you were redeemed from the
empty way of life handed down to you from your
forefathers,*

*but with the precious blood of Christ, a lamb
without blemish or defect.*

The complete deliverance that Peter proclaimed is
"ready to be revealed" in the Most Holy Place. The
fulness of our inheritance is there in the heavenlies. The
Feast of Tabernacles is breaking upon us. We must not
transfer to our children and grandchildren an "empty
way of life," the traditions of men (Mark 7:13).

"But, Brother Varner, what about Heaven?" Heaven is
a real place; it is the realm of God, and God is a Spirit.
Heaven is closer than we think (Ps. 115:16; John 4:24;
Heb. 11:39-12:2, 22-24). Someone said, "Earth is crammed
with Heaven, and every bush is aflame with the fire of

God. But only those who see take off their shoes; **the rest** just pick the berries."

Gen. 28:16-17, KJV:

> *And Jacob awaked out of his sleep, and he said, Surely the Lord is in this place; and I knew it not.*
>
> *And he was afraid, and said, How dreadful is this place! this is none other but the house of God, and this is the gate of heaven.*

Gen. 28:16-17, NIV:

> *When Jacob awoke from his sleep, he thought, "Surely the Lord is in this place, and I was not aware of it."*
>
> *He was afraid and said, "How awesome is this place! This is none other than the house of God; this is the gate of heaven."*

John 3:13, KJV:

> *And no man hath ascended up to heaven, but he that came down from heaven, even the Son of man which is in heaven.*

Every Christian is an heir of God and a joint-heir with Jesus Christ. The Head of the family died and left something to His seed. The Greek word for "inheritance" is *kleronomos*, taken from *kleros*, which has to do with the distribution and apportioning of a thing, and from *nomos*, which means "law" and is transliterated into the English word "name." Through Jesus Christ we have been given a glorious inheritance: He has assigned a portion of His great Name, of Himself, to each of us! The Tabernacle of David, a picture of the Church, was revealed to be "a people for His name" (Acts 15:14). Together we comprise His Church, His Body, a Corporate Man, "the fulness of Him that filleth all in all" (Eph. 1:20-23). You and I must show and tell the next generation everything we know about these true riches.

Luke 16:11-12, KJV:

> *If therefore ye have not been faithful in the unrighteous mammon, who will commit to your trust the true riches?*
>
> *And if ye have not been faithful in that which is another man's, who shall give you that which is your own?*

Luke 16:11, NIV:

> *So if you have not been trustworthy in handling worldly wealth, who will trust you with true riches?*
>
> *And if you have not been trustworthy with someone else's property, who will give you property of your own?*

Doctor Luke makes it clear that God will not trust us with our Father's spiritual riches until we are faithful in handling His corporate assets. We must become good stewards of His money. The New Testament has plenty to say about God's money; if preachers are afraid to talk about it, God isn't. Here are some interesting facts from the field of biblical economics:

1. *The Gospels contain more warnings against the misuse of money than any other subject.*

2. *One in every four verses in Matthew, Mark and Luke deals with money.*

3. *One in every six verses in the New Testament as a whole deals with or makes reference to money in some way.*

4. *Almost half of the parables of Jesus refer to money, particularly warning against covetousness.*

5. *The first apostle to fall was Judas; he sinned because of the love of money. He sold Jesus for money that he never lived to spend (John 12:4-8, 13:27; Acts 1:25).*

6. *The first sin the early Church concerned the giving of money to the Lord. Note how satan entered the scene when the spirit of giving was on the people (Acts 5:1-10).*

7. *The sin of "simony" concerns money and seeking to buy the gifts of God with it (Acts 8:14-24).*

Volumes could be written on this subject because giving, whether it be the giving of our finances or the giving forth of the substance and the Christ-life within, is based upon a nature: the new nature of the new creation man, created after Him in true righteousness and holiness. God is a Giver. He has to be. His nature requires it. The law of love is giving.

John 3:16, KJV:

For God so loved the world, that he gave his only begotten Son, that whosoever believeth in him should not perish, but have everlasting life.

There are two kinds of people on the planet: givers and takers. In fact, there are but two men on the planet: Christ and Adam, beauty and the beast (Song 1:5). Adam, the old man, is a beast. He is selfish. He loves money and lets it use him, being possessed by his possessions. Christ is the comely One. He is unselfish. He uses money, possessing His possessions.

Jesus Christ is the legal Owner of all things in Heaven, on earth and under the earth. All things are His, and He desires to share this glory with the Church. Someone replies, "But God will not share His glory with another." That's true, but His Church is not another! We are bone of His bone and flesh of His flesh. Like husband and wife, Christ and his Church are heirs together of the grace of life (Eph. 5:22-33, I Pet. 3:7). Our heavenly Boaz is a mighty man of wealth (Ruth 2:1).

Phil. 4:19, KJV:

But my God shall supply all your need according to his riches in glory by Christ Jesus.

Eph. 2:11-12, KJV:

Wherefore remember, that ye being in time past Gentiles in the flesh, who are called Uncircumcision by that which is called the Circumcision in the flesh made by hands;

That at that time ye were without Christ, being aliens from the commonwealth of Israel, and strangers from the covenants of promise, having no hope, and without God in the world...

The Church is the Israel of God (Gal. 3:29, 6:16). We are part of His commonwealth, and have His wealth in common. But here is the difference: God's wealth is wealth that is to be given away; He blesses us that we might bless others. God is a Giver and His people are all givers. This giving must be...

1. *Systematic—Give your tithes and offerings when you get paid.*

2. *Sacrificial—Be ready to give more than usual at times.*

3. *Spontaneous—Always be open to the voice of the Holy Ghost.*

4. *Spiritual—Let your principles and motives be Bible-based.*

Tithing in the Realm of the Body

Now that the foundations of stewardship are laid, we are ready to discuss the taboo topic of tithing. The word for "tithe" in Hebrew is *mah-as-raw* (Strong's #4643) and means "a tenth, a tithe." It is traced back to the root word *aw-shar* (#6238) which means "to accumulate; to grow rich." The Greek root word is *dekate* (#1181) and means "a tenth." Note that tithing was...

1. *Before the law—Gen. 14:18-20, 28:20-22.*

2. *Under the law—Lev. 27:30-33; Num. 18:20-32; Deut. 12:5-17; 14:22-28; 26:12; II Chron. 31:5-12; Neh. 10:37-39; 12:44; 13:5, 10-12; Amos 4:4; Mal. 3:8-12.*

3. *After the law—Matt. 23:23; Luke 11:42, 18:12; Heb. 7:1-21.*

Mal. 3:8-12, KJV:

Will a man rob God? Yet ye have robbed me. But ye say, Wherein have we robbed thee? In tithes and offerings.

*Ye **are** cursed with a curse: for ye have robbed me, **even** this whole nation.*

*Bring ye all the tithes into the storehouse, that there may be meat in mine house, and prove me now herewith, saith the Lord of hosts, if I will not open you the windows of heaven, and pour you out a blessing, that **there shall** not **be room** enough **to receive it.***

And I will rebuke the devourer for your sakes, and he shall not destroy the fruits of your ground; neither shall your vine cast her fruit before the time in the field, saith the Lord of hosts.

And all nations shall call you blessed: for ye shall be a delightsome land, saith the Lord of hosts.

The whole tithe is to be brought to the storehouse, the local church where you are being fed. If you are not being fed, move. If you can't flow, go.

Examine verse 10 of the above passage and remove the all bold words (added by the translators). The result is interestingly brief: "that not enough . . . " What does this mean? There is a two-fold promise in this passage:

1. *God will open the windows of Heaven.*

2. *God will pour out a blessing so great that there is not room enough to receive it.*

The giving of the tithe opens the window! What comes through the window is the blessing. It is determined by the offering given in addition to the tithe, and can come in spoonfuls or truckloads. This explains why some folks who only tithe have yet to receive an abundance. Open the window and start offering. As for thieves, a "bag with holes" is their portion (Hag. 1:1-5). Giving the tithe is not enough.

What does it mean to tithe in the realm of the body? This is Outer Court tithing, the tithe in the natural realm. This has to do with the common notion of tithing, the giving of a tenth of our finances. Even baby Christians can give this natural tithe. It is milk and a basic act of obedience to the Word. Let me reduce my teaching on this subject to the simplest terms: Christians tithe, thieves don't. Christians tithe, and the Bible has promised much to the man who is liberal in his giving.

Prov. 3:9-10, KJV:

Honour the Lord with thy substance, and with the firstfruits of all thine increase:

So shall thy barns be filled with plenty, and thy presses shall burst out with new wine.

Luke 6:38, KJV:

Give, and it shall be given unto you; good measure, pressed down, and shaken together, and running over, shall men give into your bosom. For with the same measure that ye mete withal it shall be measured to you again.

II Cor. 9:6-7, KJV:

But this I say, He which soweth sparingly shall reap also sparingly; and he which soweth bountifully shall reap also bountifully.

Every man according as he purposeth in his heart, so let him give; not grudgingly, or of necessity: for God loveth a cheerful giver.

The Bible teaches us how to give. We must give willingly (Ex. 35:22). Paul's admonition in First Corinthians 16:2 reveals that our giving must be regular ("upon the first day of the week"), personal ("let every one of you"), and proportional ("as God hath prospered him"). One's giving should be according to his income or ability (Deut. 16:17; Prov. 3:27-28; Acts 11:29; II Cor. 8:12, 9:6). Christians should give freely (Matt. 10:8). God loves a cheerful, literally, a "hilarious" giver (II Cor. 9:7), just like Himself. May He help us to give with simplicity, sincerity, and generosity (Rom. 12:8). May our motives ever be proper (I Chron. 29:3, Matt. 6:1-4). God's priests are always ready to bless. His hand has opened to us and now we throw wide our hand to others (Deut. 15:7-11).

As we conclude this segment on elementary tithing, somebody asks, "Pastor Varner, do I tithe before or after taxes? On the net or on the gross? Before taxes, my check would be for $49.18 and after taxes it would be $37.02." Don't bother, child. Keep the change. You still think that it's your money.

Tithing in the Realm of the Soul

Mark 12:41, KJV:

> *And Jesus sat over against the treasury, and beheld how the people cast money into the treasury: and many that were rich cast in much.*

Tithing in the realm of the body has to do with our finances. Next, Holy Place tithing in the realm of the soul takes into account our attitude, our mentality. With what mindset do we give? How do we give? Be careful. Jesus is watching. He is the One who taught about this second dimension of tithing. Our heavenly Executive Company Officer, the Head of the Corporation (His Body), validated the natural tithe, and then directed us to give something along with our money.

Matt. 23:23, KJV:

> *Woe unto you, scribes and Pharisees, hypocrites! for ye pay tithe of mint and anise and cummin, and have omitted the weightier matters of the law, judgment, mercy, and faith: these ought ye to have done, and not to leave the other undone.*

Matt. 23:23, NIV:

> *Woe to you, teachers of the law and Pharisees, you hypocrites! You give a tenth of your spices—mint, dill and cummin. But you have neglected the more important matters of the law—justice, mercy and faithfulness. You should have practiced the latter, without neglecting the former.*

It is significant that Jesus linked these "weightier matters" with the subject of tithing. Why? Because they speak of giving. It is noteworthy that the word "judgment" used here is the Greek word *krisis* which is in the feminine gender, and speaks of the realm of the soul or the mind.

It is far easier to give our finances than to give justice, mercy and faith. Jesus endorsed the financial tithe here when He said, "You should have practiced the latter." For those who want to nit-pick the issue of tithing in the New Testament, be informed that 10% is a good place to start on the way to real New Testament giving—100%!

May His mind freely operate in us as we minister judgment and justice as He would give it. This is correction unto righteousness, not the abomination of condemnation (Prov. 17:15). It takes real giving of oneself to patiently lift up another into the way of righteousness; it is easier for folks to cast a scornful eye and pronounce judgment against the situation. The first covenant was a ministration of condemnation unto death (II Cor. 3-4). The blood of Jesus is better blood, crying for mercy from the heavens. This is far nobler than the blood of Abel that cries for vengeance from the dust of the lower nature. Jesus Himself exemplified tithing in the soul.

Matt. 12:20, KJV:

A bruised reed shall he not break, and smoking flax shall he not quench, till he send forth judgment unto victory.

Matt. 12:20, NIV:

A bruised reed he will not break, and a smoldering wick he will not snuff out, till he leads justice to victory.

A new priesthood has caught the vision of the Mercy-seat. These freely give themselves and their treasure to the Lord, not to mention plenty of justice, mercy and faith in His Name. Gifts of the soul ought to be given as well as the tithing of the material things with which we are blessed.

Tithing in the Realm of Spirit

Thirdly, tithing in the realm of spirit interfaces the Most Holy Place and the Melchisedec Priesthood. Remember that this third dimension has to do with nature and being. We now move from the religious to the real, from shadow to essence. The righteous remnant becomes the tithe, a tithe company, a people who become what they give.

Isa. 6:11-13, KJV:

Then said I, Lord, how long? And he answered, Until the cities be wasted without inhabitant, and the houses without man, and the land be utterly desolate,

And the Lord have removed men far away, and there be a great forsaking in the midst of the land.

But yet in it shall be a tenth, and it shall return, and shall be eaten: as a teil tree, and as an oak, whose substance is in them, when they cast their leaves: so the holy seed shall be the substance thereof.

Lev. 27:32, KJV:

And concerning the tithe of the herd, or of the flock, even of whatsoever passeth under the rod, the tenth shall be holy unto the Lord.

The tithe is holy. This tithe company is a holy seed. The substance within them is the Christ (Col. 1:27). These are a firstfruits unto God and the Lamb (Rev. 14:1-5), a people who have been stripped of everything, like an oak tree which loses all its leaves in the fall and winter. The *Goodspeed* translation of Isaiah 6:13 says that this tithe "must pass through the fire again." This is the baptism of fire in the Most Holy Place. A royal seed becomes a whole burnt offering, a people who have become His tithe.

This tithe company also passes "under the rod." This new priesthood has come under His authority and the rule of His Kingdom. The scepter of His Kingdom is a rod of righteousness, a shepherd's staff which governs, guards and guides. The tithe company is a covenantal people. Read the prophecies of Isaiah, Jeremiah and Zechariah, and you will meet this same people, the corporate man whose name is the Branch.

Luke 17:11-19, NIV:

Now on his way to Jerusalem, Jesus traveled along the border between Samaria and Galilee.

As he was going into a village, ten men who had leprosy met him. They stood at a distance

and called out in a loud voice, "Jesus, Master, have pity on us!"

When he saw them, he said, "Go, show yourselves to the priests." And as they went, they were cleansed.

One of them, when he saw he was healed, came back, praising God in a loud voice.

He threw himself at Jesus' feet and thanked him— and he was a Samaritan.

Jesus asked, "Were not all ten cleansed? Where are the other nine?

Was no one found to return and give praise to God except this foreigner?"

Then he said to him, "Rise and go; your faith has made you well." WHOLE

Luke 17:18, KJV:

There are not found that returned to give glory to God, save this stranger.

The priests who become His tithe in the Most Holy Place are the people of Hosea 6:1-3 who return to the Lord. Ten lepers were cleansed; the tithe, one out of ten, returned to give Him glory, and like Ruth of old, to throw himself at the Master's feet. This priesthood after the order of Melchisedec is from the tribe of Judah, which means "praise." We are not ashamed, afraid, or embarrassed to honor our King with a "loud voice." He has cleansed us from the leprosy of sin and made us sit with Him in heavenly places (Eph. 2:1-6).

Num. 18:26-28, KJV:

Thus speak unto the Levites, and say unto them, When ye take of the children of Israel the tithes which I have given you from them for your inheritance, then ye shall offer up an heave offering of it for the Lord, even a tenth part of the tithe.

And this your heave offering shall be reckoned unto you, as though it were the corn of the threshingfloor, and as the fulness of the winepress.

Thus ye also shall offer an heave offering unto the Lord of all your tithes, which ye receive of the children of Israel; and ye shall give thereof the Lord's heave offering to Aaron the priest.

Isa. 53:6, KJV:

All we like sheep have gone astray; we have turned every one to his own way; and the Lord hath laid on him the iniquity of us all.

Matt. 18:12, KJV:

How think ye? if a man have an hundred sheep, and one of them be gone astray, doth he not leave the ninety and nine, and goeth into the mountains, and seeketh that which is gone astray?

The tenth of the tenth, the tithe of the tithe, belonged to Aaron the High Priest. The Lord Jesus, our Great High Priest, is also the Good Shepherd. He gave His life for all the sheep, but at this season He is looking and searching out one in a hundred, a tithe of the tithe, His portion and His alone. He combs the mountains and kingdoms for a people of worship, and brings "one of a city, and two of a family" (Jer. 3:14) to Mount Zion, to stand with Him in full redemption.

To summarize, there is the giving of a tenth of our increase in material goods as we give cheerfully and joyfully unto the Lord. There is also the giving of justice, mercy and faith as we give with the right attitude. Supremely, there is the realm of full giving wherein a priesthood has been changed. In the Most Holy Place, we become God's tithe, a people wholly given to be His delight and pleasure. To this priesthood the Lord says, "I will not only open the windows of Heaven for you; I will open you and make you to become the floodgates of Heaven. I will not only pour out an abundant blessing for you; I will pour you out and make you to become the blessing that is immeasurable and inestimable. I will open *you*; I will pour *you* out."

Take or Receive?

This chapter is longer than planned; that we cut it short reveals the importance of the Money Principle. Once we are caught up beyond the lesser realms of finance, once we have seen Him who is seated between the cherubim, once we glimpse the vision of a people who will become His tithe, little else need be said about the way preachers should take offerings. I'm going to do to you what Paul did. After unveiling the glories of the resurrection in First Corinthians 15, he opened the next chapter by bluntly saying, "Now concerning the collection . . ."

Heb. 7:5-6, KJV:

And verily they that are of the sons of Levi, who receive the office of the priesthood, have a commandment to take tithes of the people according to the law, that is, of their brethren, though they come out of the loins of Abraham:

> *But he whose descent is not counted from them received tithes of Abraham, and blessed him that had the promises.*

The old order takes tithes. The royal priesthood is a blessing order and receives tithes. Contained in the verses above is the conclusion to this chapter. They also hold the most powerful incentive for believers to pay tithes to Jesus — we are convinced that He is alive! Folks who don't tithe must not believe that He rose from the dead, or that His interest rate for unpaid tithes is 20% (Lev. 27:31)! Above all others, the thieves should be glad for a change of priesthood; they can let one of us remit their sin so they can be delivered and stop stealing from God. If they continue to ignore that kind of mercy, they will have to answer to the One they violated, the Savior who is also their Judge. And every man has his day in court (Rom. 14:12).

Suffice it to say that God is about to flush all the extortioners, and then give the wealth of the nations to a responsible priesthood who will, like the dynamic duo of Joshua and Eleazer (the king-priest principle), cause others to inherit.

I don't want to waste your time or mine, so I won't lower us into any lengthy considerations about the contemporary practices of multi-offerings, marathon offerings, auctions, "the biggest bill in your wallet" offerings, pledges, ad nauseum; not to mention all the parachurch bandits who violate the authority of the local church as they unashamedly plunder the saints with blessing pacts, prosperity plans, threats ("the devil is attacking this ministry and is trying to shut us down"), guilt trips ("you must give or souls will go to hell") . . . all of these abominations have piled up into one huge mound of dung. Like Nehemiah (whose name means "Comforter"), the Holy Ghost is beginning to pick up this mess and, like a heavenly bulldozer, push it where it belongs . . . outside the camp. It's like the time when Jesus went to town to attend the national convention and ended up tipping tables.

Neh. 4:10, NIV:

> *Meanwhile, the people in Judah said, "The strength of the laborers is giving out, and there is so much rubble that we cannot rebuild the wall."*

Matt. 21:12-13, KJV:

> *And Jesus went into the temple of God, and cast out all them that sold and bought in the temple, and overthrew the tables of the moneychangers, and the seats of them that sold doves,*
>
> *And said unto them, It is written, My house shall be called the house of prayer; but ye have made it a den of thieves.*

The priesthood is changing, and so is everything we thought we knew about finances. There is a priesthood in the earth who simply receive from the Lord. No sweat. We pray and obey. We have learned that prosperity means that we always have enough, and such godliness with contentment is great gain. Only His grace has brought us to this day.

This new priesthood cannot be bought or bribed; don't even think about it. We are not into spiritual pimpery and prostitution. We are not peddling our wares. We stopped drugging the saints with false hopes years ago; their trip has been cancelled. We don't need a bookie because we left Egypt and stopped playing the horses. We don't contract for our services. We are not for sale.

Everyone wants this new kid on the block, but everyone has a problem. Local churches and believers everywhere desperately need and desire the Christ-life within this new priest, but the same Spirit within him is also publishing the death-knell to every kingdom but the Lord's. This new ministry is not afraid of men or impressed with what they have built. We care about what others say about us. We have feelings, but what men say and how they say it, blessings or cursings, will not and cannot move us. The priesthood is changing, and the new Man is under exclusive covenantal rights to the One who sent him. King Jesus is in control.

Chapter 14

The Management Principle

Who's in Charge?

Our closing concerns are twofold: summary and application. What have you learned? What are you going to do with it? How do you get started? The Management Principle is very personal . . . I want to speak to your heart. As a teacher, I never assume anything, but if you've hung with me this far, you're either part of a changing priesthood or extremely curious. Whichever, let's do a quick review, noting the essence of each chapter.

Phil. 3:1, NIV:

> *Finally, my brothers, rejoice in the Lord! It is no trouble for me to write the same things to you again, and it is a safeguard for you.*

Chapter One briefly reviewed excellent things (Prov. 22:20) or threefold things. This truth is detailed in two other books, *Prevail* and *The More Excellent Ministry*. The first chapter emphasized one major point: There is a dimension beyond our spiritual adolescence, there is something more than the Feast of Pentecost and the Holy Place realm — the Feast of Tabernacles and the Most Holy Place realm.

Chapter Two encouraged us to draw near to this new thing (Heb. 10:19-22). Men are always fearful of the unknown, especially if they have a reputation to uphold and a kingdom to maintain. We are passing over and need not shrink back in fear. Whichever direction you go and whatever path you take, please don't take issue with what you don't understand.

Chapter Three showed us that God takes away the old with violence so that the new can be established (Heb. 10:9). Jesus isn't going to play patty-cake with His Church in the 1990s. He is not taking sides these days, especially over moot points of theology or eschatology. He is for Himself. Get ready for some powerful changes.

Chapter Four is a challenge to all those to whom has been committed the Word of God, those who have experienced a circumcision of heart (Rom. 3:1-2). The season has already begun for God to come to the Jew first. He's going to the Gentiles next, and when He pours out this revelation on the Outer Court, there won't be enough priests to handle the crowds of both Jew and Greek. After the apostle, prophet, evangelist, pastor and teacher movements, God is going to have a saints' movement.

Chapter Five overviewed and introduced the remaining nine chapters, each of which is a practical part of this changing priesthood.

Chapter Six, "The Melchisedec Principle," taught us to shift our point of view from the future to the present,

to see as God sees (Phil. 3:20). The Son is here, flowing
from the Mercy-seat with His present priesthood. An
overcoming Church is seated and ministering with Him.

Chapter Seven, "The Measure Principle," showed the
difference between duality and singleness (James 1:22-
25). Doublemindedness is idolatry. We left Adam and
satan in the Holy Place and now focus only on the glory
of God revealed in the face of Jesus Christ, the Man in
the Mirror.

Chapter Eight, "The Marriage Principle," brought
healing to sheep damaged by the extremes of dis-
cipleship. It explained the liberating truth that all
authority and submission is under the curse (Eph. 5:30-
33). In order to have obedience, two wills are required.
God's ultimate intention is not our obedience, but our
union with Him. We must keep all things in perspective,
knowing the differences between the passing and the
permanent.

Chapter Nine, "The Mouthpiece Principle," is perhaps the most relevant one in this volume. God is speaking a greater emphasis than that placed upon mere
prophets: Jesus, the Prophet (Heb. 1:1). We are becoming
deaf to the voices of the many as we are being gathered
by the Voice of One. Our spirits are only open to the
sound of Him and those whom He sends in His Name.
We are not gathering unto body or soul, but unto spirit
. . . unto Him.

Chapter Ten, "The Mountain Principle," is the fifth of
these nine points. From Sinai and a priesthood which
cannot be touched, we are moving to Zion and a ministry
which is accessible, transparent and secure in Christ

(Heb. 12:18-24). We are part of a city without walls, a city of clean, clear glass.

Chapter Eleven, "The Man Principle," showed the difference between healing and the Healer. God is healing us completely, in spirit, soul and body (I Thess. 5:23). He is raising us up in the third day to live in His sight. God will heal the nations.

Chapter Twelve, "The Motive Principle," probed us and searched our hearts. Are we seeking God's hand, what He has done, His presents; or are we seeking God's face, who He is, His Presence (Matt. 6:33)? We must not seek His hand in the realm of the body or the soul; we must seek His face in the realm of the spirit. We have experienced thanksgiving and praise, but are now standing in the Most Holy Place, the greatest place, the place of worship.

Chapter Thirteen, "The Money Principle," revealed the importance of biblical economics. Levi takes tithes, but Melchisedec receives tithes (Heb. 7:5-6). Tithing is in three dimensions: body, soul and spirit. We are becoming His tithe, a tithe company in the Most Holy Place.

The Issue Is Always Governmental

Now we come to the last chapter; or is it the first? "The Management Principle" underscores the application of all that we have learned. These truths must be practiced and performed; they must impact our daily living, else we join the ranks of the armchair theologians who are useless to the Kingdom of God.

The bottom line is this: Who's in charge? Is it God or the devil, Adam or Christ, man or God? Are you in control or is Jesus in control? Who has the reins, the rudder? Who's driving and where are we going? That's the issue. It's a governmental one. It always has been.

Let me encourage my fellow pastors. No one ever skipped out the back door of your local church over doctrine or any other reason they told you; that was just a smokescreen. The real reason was governmental (I am assuming that you are a godly pastor, preaching the Word and lifting up Jesus). Those people left because they could not be in charge. Like Saul, they had invaded the priesthood.

I Sam. 15:22-23, KJV:

> And Samuel said, Hath the Lord as great delight in burnt offerings and sacrifices, as in obeying the voice of the Lord? Behold, to obey is better than sacrifice, and to hearken than the fat of rams.

> For rebellion is as the sin of witchcraft, and stubbornness is as iniquity and idolatry. Because thou hast rejected the word of the Lord, he hath also rejected thee from being king.

The most damnable thing we face in the ministry is this: people quote the Bible, appearing to speak the things of the Spirit, but are actually speaking out of their soul (their own reasoning based on circumstantial, sensory knowledge) to justify their actions. All the while they are deluded, supposing that they have heard from God. They use the Scriptures to substantiate their own stubbornness, the musings of the beast. These people learned this game from the kind of preachers who would take the third day principles of this book to prop up their own second day agenda.

This mixture comes out in the most hellish form, not a request for prayer, but an announcement: "God told me . . . God said it. I know He did." It was god who spoke, all right: the god of this world, the god of the cosmos, which is the order, system and arrangement of things between a man's ears (the way he thinks, his arrangement of concepts and ideas). What we think, feel or want is usually the god who speaks what we want to hear.

Then, as if to convince himself, this same person adds, "I just know that it's God, pastor. I feel such peace!" What you feel, my dear, is not peace in your spirit, but relief in your soul. You want to be in charge. You have taken matters into you own hands and delivered yourself from that which was pressuring you to change! You said, "Move over, Jesus, I am going to rule today." There you sit, perched in your own cockiness, defying the Lord or any of His messengers. The days of your kingdom are numbered.

Please, dear one, don't count me your enemy. I am your friend and your brother. I have been sent to you in the Name of the One who is King and Boss. There is no "plan B." He is the covenantal God. Everything is the way He says that it is, every shot the way He calls it. All things are done on His terms and in His time, His way. You can accept that or reject it, but you cannot alter it.

It's easy to know if God has really spoken to you; proving that is quite simple. A word from God, the word of the Lord, can be confronted and challenged by a brother or a true friend, and you won't get spooked,

touchy or upset. If it's God, it will stand, it will keep. But
if that word came out of the spirit of man or the devil,
you'll get mean and nasty when cornered, and get the
urge to run, especially from the one who questioned that
word.

Men want to be in charge. This last chapter is the most
important of all. You can memorize this whole book. You
can crawl into my peanut-sized brain and draw out all I
know or all that you think I know, and still miss it. We
will not and cannot deliver the groaning creation on the
basis of what we know. We can only be a blessing to
others on the basis of who we are in union with Jesus
Christ, and He is in charge.

God Doesn't Need Your Help

Heb. 4:7-11, NIV:

*Therefore God again set a certain day, calling it
Today, when a long time later he spoke through David,
as was said before: "Today, if you hear his voice, do not
harden your hearts."*

*For if Joshua had given them rest, God would not
have spoken later about another day.*

*There remains, then, a Sabbath-rest for the people of
God;*

*for anyone who enters God's rest also rests from his
own work, just as God did from his.*

*Let us, therefore, make every effort to enter that rest,
so that no one will fall by following their example of disobedience.*

Heb. 4:11, KJV:

Let us labour therefore to enter into that rest, lest any man fall after the same example of unbelief.

That Day is here: the seventh day from Adam and the third day from Jesus. The hardest thing for a man to do is nothing. God doesn't need our help. We are finally coming to the end of our wisdom and strength, the cessation of our own works, that we might rest in His. The greatest obstacle facing this new priesthood is the determination of others to try to make it happen, help it happen or explain why it is happening. Pastor, the last thing you need is a good idea. Our preconceptions, previous teachings, and wide range of experience and plans will have to go on the altar. The Ark is coming home to rest.

1 Chron. 13:1-3, NIV:

David conferred with each of his officers, the commanders of thousands and commanders of hundreds.

He then said to the whole assembly of Israel, "If it seems good to you and if it is the will of the Lord our God, let us send word far and wide to the rest of our brothers throughout the territories of Israel, and also to the priests and Levites who are with them in their towns and pasturelands, to come and join us.

Let us bring the ark of our God back to us, for we did not inquire of it during the reign of Saul."

1 Chron. 13:7-10, NIV:

They moved the ark of God from Abinadab's house on a new cart, with Uzzah and Ahio guiding it.

*David and all the Israelites were celebrating with all
their might before God, with songs and with harps,
lyres, tambourines, cymbals and trumpets.*

*When they came to the threshing floor of Kidon,
Uzzah reached out his hand to steady the ark, because
the oxen stumbled.*

*The Lord's anger burned against Uzzah, and he
struck him down because he had put his hand on the
ark. So he died there before God.*

God killed Uzzah. His name means "strength, might,
power, firmness, splendor, majesty, and glory." Ahio, his
brother, was also driving the cart. His name means
"brother or brotherly." This national gathering seemed
brotherly, for all the big-name preachers were there.
When the oxen stumbled, Uzzah touched the glory of
God with the "strength" of man. His motive was pure:
he was trying to keep the thing in balance; the abomination was that the thing itself was demon-inspired, not according to God's prescribed pattern. A study of the sixth
chapter of First Samuel will show that a "new cart" was
a Philistine invention, a manmade method of bringing
back the Ark. Carts have wheels, go in circles, and make
ruts. A rut is a grave with both ends knocked out.

I Chron. 15:13-15, KJV:

*For because ye did it not at the first, the Lord our
God made a breach upon us, for that we sought him not
after the due order.*

*So the priests and the Levites sanctified themselves
to bring up the ark of the Lord God of Israel.*

> *And the children of the Levites bare the ark of God upon their shoulders with the staves thereon, as Moses commanded according to the word of the Lord.*

1 Chron. 15:13, NIV:

> *It was because you, the Levites, did not bring it up the first time that the Lord our God broke out in anger against us. We did not inquire of him about how to do it in the prescribed way.*

The priesthood is changing. We must uphold the glory of God, the Lordship of Jesus, and do everything according to the pattern our King has ordained. Man's strength will not be able to stand in the Day of the Lord. Man will lose control during the third day. Make it easy on yourself. Stop struggling. Hand over the reins of your heart and seek Him after the due order. Kneel at the cross, and Christ will meet you there.

Have You Fallen Through the Grate Yet?

The brazen altar in the Tabernacle of Moses was like a barbecue pit. It was made of wood, covered with brass and had a strong, grated network on the inside. It was not a pretty place. There were blood and guts everywhere. It smelled bad. The savour of death filled the air of the Outer Court. That blood-stained altar pointed to the cross of Jesus Christ, a gruesome picture, ghastly to behold. Crucifixion was the worst and most shameful of deaths. There was no beauty in Him that we should desire Him (Isa. 53:1-2).

Isa. 52:14-15, NIV:

> *Just as there were many who were appalled at him— his appearance was so disfigured beyond that of any man and his form marred beyond human likeness—*

> *so will he sprinkle many nations, and kings will shut their mouths because of him. For what they were not told, they will see, and what they have not heard, they will understand.*

Gal. 3:13-14, NIV:

> *Christ redeemed us from the curse of the law by becoming a curse for us, for it is written: "Cursed is everyone who is hung on a tree."*

> *He redeemed us in order that the blessing given to Abraham might come to the Gentiles through Christ Jesus, so that by faith we might receive the promise of the Spirit.*

Two crosses have been predetermined for your death: His and yours. The way of the cross is the way to Zion. The crucified life is not an option. The grated network within the brazen altar was strong, showing that you cannot escape your dying to self. You must be broken before the Lord and dealt with. Only then can He sprinkle you upon the nations.

Ps. 118:27, KJV:

> *God is the Lord, which hath shewed us light: bind the sacrifice with cords, even unto the horns of the altar.*

Have you fallen through the grate yet? It's supper time, time for the Feast of Tabernacles, the main meal. Don't sip, sup (Rev. 3:20). Don't pick at your plate. The menu includes barbecued you. You can come like a stuck pig or a little lamb, but you must come. God can tie you down or you can just lie quietly; He has two ways to cook a priest: the "tie" method or the "lie" method. The fire of God, the Word of God, must ignite the sacrifice. When you have been completely consumed, you will fall through the grate. The last thing to drop through is your head.

The Hebrew word for the whole burnt offering, or ascending offering, is *olah*, and is in the same word family as *El-elyon*, "Most High God." The Most High God is the God of the Most Holy Place and is the name for God associated with Melchisedec. The Latin form of *olah* is *holacausta*. There is a people in the earth who are allowing the Lord to completely engulf every part of their lives. These are becoming a whole burnt offering unto the Lord, a kingdom of priests (Ex. 19:1-6) who are not afraid of the furnace of affliction. These are being wholly devoured by the Word of the Lord and are falling through the grate. These priests are submitting to His reducing them and everything that concerns them to ashes. But He will give us beauty for ashes!

Isa. 61:3, KJV:

...To appoint unto them that mourn in Zion, to give unto them beauty for ashes, the oil of joy for mourning, the garment of praise for the spirit of heaviness; that they might be called trees of righteousness, the planting of the Lord, that he might be glorified.

Isa. 61:3, NIV:

...and provide for those who grieve in Zion—to bestow on them a crown of beauty instead of ashes, the oil of gladness instead of mourning, and a garment of praise instead of a spirit of despair. They will be called

oaks of righteousness, a planting of the Lord for the display of his splendor.

A Priest With Urim and Thummim

Ezra 2:61-63, KJV:

And of the children of the priests: the children of Habaiah, the children of Koz, the children of Barzillai; which took a wife of the daughters of Barzillai the Gileadite, and was called after their name:

These sought their register among those that were reckoned by genealogy, but they were not found: therefore were they, as polluted, put from the priesthood.

And the Tirshatha said unto them, that they should not eat of the most holy things, till there stood up a priest with Urim and with Thummim.

A many-membered priest is standing up. He has Urim ("lights") and Thummim ("perfections"). He has an understanding of perfection, of how God will complete His purposes. The Temple is being rebuilt, the time is come to eat "the most holy things" of the Most Holy Place. We have done that together in this volume. Thank you for dining with me.

During this last supper some, like Judas, are being thrown out of the restaurant, put away from the priesthood. These ministries are polluted because the writing cannot be found which validates the Seed. Their hearts are an empty slate. Weighed in the balances and found wanting, these priests have always done God's will their way, but no longer.

Serious times are here. God is bothering all of us. He's so unpredictable now; He's not acting at all like He's supposed to. Under pressure (from God, not the devil), we've quoted the Word, we've bound and loosed, and then loosed and bound. You know what I mean? Mark it down. Settle it now. From here on, none of us are going to sail into waters of our own choosing. The wind of the Holy Ghost has caught our ship (Acts 27), changing the course of the priesthood.

Like the prophet of old, we have ventured into the depths (Ezek. 47:1-12). Jump in or slink back to the edge of the river. The handwriting is on the wall (Dan. 5), but nobody can read it. The magicians and soothsayers of Babylon are helpless, about to call for Daniel. The prophets of Jezebel are (as we say in the south) "wore slam out"; meanwhile, Elijah waits his turn. What a strange hour! Who can tell us what in the world is going on?

Job 33:23-25, KJV:

If there be a messenger with him, an interpreter, one among a thousand, to shew unto man his uprightness:

Then he is gracious unto him, and saith, Deliver him from going down to the pit: I have found a ransom.

His flesh shall be fresher than a child's: he shall return to the days of his youth...

Song 6:8-9, KJV:

There are threescore queens, and fourscore concubines, and virgins without number.

> *My dove, my undefiled is but one; she is the only one of her mother, she is the choice one of her that bare her. The daughters saw her, and blessed her; yea, the queens and the concubines, and they praised her.*

One among a thousand. An interpreter, a messenger, a bringer of hope to a dying world. I have found a Ransom. Have you? I want more than anything to be part of a priesthood that is changing. I want to declare His righteousness. I know my purpose as I stand with those who are laying the foundation for the third feast. I pray in Jesus' Name that His present purposes are being built into you and your family so that you may arise, taking your place in the priesthood that has been changed.

His Name is John

Luke 1:57-67, KJV:

> *Now Elisabeth's full time came that she should be delivered; and she brought forth a son.*
>
> *And her neighbours and her cousins heard how the Lord had shewed great mercy upon her; and they rejoiced with her.*
>
> *And it came to pass, that on the eighth day they came to circumcise the child; and they called him Zacharias, after the name of his father.*
>
> *And his mother answered and said, Not so; but he shall be called John.*
>
> *And they said unto her, There is none of thy kindred that is called by this name.*

And they made signs to his father, how he would have him called.

And he asked for a writing table, and wrote, saying, His name is John. And they marvelled all.

And his mouth was opened immediately, and his tongue loosed, and he spake, and praised God.

And fear came on all that dwelt round about them: and all these sayings were noised abroad throughout all the hill country of Judaea.

And all they that heard them laid them up in their hearts, saying, What manner of child shall this be! And the hand of the Lord was with him.

And his father Zacharias was filled with the Holy Ghost, and prophesied...

The fulness of time has come; it's time for the child, the new thing, to be named or natured. This act is to be done by his father on the eighth day. All the neighbors and cousins are here; every camp is represented. Each is decked to the hilt with his own preconceived notions, his witty inventions. Each has his own prophet, primed and ready to confirm standard procedure. All have one thing in common: each is devoted to telling the world that this new baby must be named Zecharias, Jr., because the tradition of the elders, not to mention their theology and eschatology, demands it.

Stand back, everybody. Zecharias has moved his hand and motioned for a writing table. What excitement! We've waited 400 years for this. The last few months

have been unbearable. Once again, there will be a prophet in the land.

But wait a minute. This cannot be. Will somebody please explain what is happening here? Who's in charge? The old priest is beginning to write, and his first letter isn't Z . . . it's J! Maybe he's forgotten how to spell. Doesn't he know the rules of spiritual grammar?

J . . . O . . . H . . . N . . . John. John . . . His name is John!

Nobody expected this. All the neighbors and cousins are shocked, and for the first time in many years, are speechless. But not Zecharias. The tongue of the obedient priest is loosed as he begins to declare the wonderful works of God.

Luke 1:68-79, KJV:

> *Blessed be the Lord God of Israel; for he hath visited and redeemed his people,*
>
> *And hath raised up an horn of salvation for us in the house of his servant David;*
>
> *As he spake by the mouth of his holy prophets, which have been since the world began:*
>
> *That we should be saved from our enemies, and from the hand of all that hate us;*
>
> *To perform the mercy promised to our fathers, and to remember his holy covenant;*
>
> *The oath which he sware to our father Abraham,*
>
> *That he would grant unto us, that we being delivered out of the hand of our enemies might serve him without fear,*

In holiness and righteousness before him, all the days of our life.

And thou, child, shalt be called the prophet of the Highest: for thou shalt go before the face of the Lord to prepare his ways;

To give knowledge of salvation unto his people by the remission of their sins,

Through the tender mercy of our God; whereby the dayspring from on high hath visited us,

To give light to them that sit in darkness and in the shadow of death, to guide our feet into the way of peace.

1990 is history. For months there has been silence. 1991 has begun. We have heard the Word of the Lord: The priesthood is changing! A new baby has been birthed and is about to be named. What must we do?

It's simple. Bring the writing table. Not the tables of stone, but the fleshly tables of your heart. Bring God something He can write on. Agree quickly with the angel, the messenger (Gal. 4:14). Say "yes" to what God has said, and He will liberate your tongue to declare the realities of the third day as He raises you up in the spirit of prophecy.

You can't figure it out, so stop trying. This revival, the greatest outpouring of the Holy Ghost that the earth has ever witnessed (Matt. 24:14), is just beginning. This new priesthood is exceeding abundantly above all you can ask or think, so it doesn't matter what you think about it. What matters most is that you have heard from Heaven and have received of His life.

Bring the writing table. Bring your heart. Be a hearer and a doer, and agree with your Father. Don't be afraid. Step forward.

The finger of the Holy Ghost has written a new word on your heart. This word is "hope." Wait just a moment. Your Father has written a postscript. It reads, "Begin again."

This time it will be different. This renaissance is new, fresh, unprecedented. His name is John . . . "God is gracious." His grace is enough. The priesthood is changing, and his name is John.

Books and Tapes
By Kelley Varner

How to Order

Your offering for the books and tapes will be used to purchase supplies, purchase and maintain equipment, and, most importantly, to send literature and tapes to ministries and saints in other nations for whom nothing has been prepared (Neh. 8:10).

TAPE CATALOG
To receive a full listing of Kelley's books and tapes, write or call for our current catalog:

> Praise Tabernacle
> P.O. Box 785
> Richlands, N.C. 28574-0785
> (919) 324-5026 or 324-5027

PREVAIL: A HANDBOOK FOR THE OVERCOMER—
published by Revival Press. Now in its 4th reprinting
since 1982. 170 pages. Three major principles: Jesus is
Priest and King, Salvation Is Progressive, and Pressing
through Tribulation. What is the balance to the "faith"
message? What is the transformation of the soul? How
are our minds being renewed? Does God want to take us
out or bring us through? This book will provide a much-
needed balance of the presentation of the foundational
truths of the Kingdom of God and will tear down many
traditional strongholds. After the Baptism of the Holy
Ghost, then what? (16 tapes available)

THE MORE EXECELLENT MINISTRY—published by
Destiny Image. 290 pages. We are standing on the threshhold of the Most Holy Place and the fullfillment of the
Feast of Tabernacles. There is a Man in the throne who now
beckons us to share His Mercy-seat. How does His ministry operate? How do we know that we are called to share
this word of reconcilation? Here are new principles for a
new day that will enable you to walk successfully during
this critical time. There is a new sound in the earth: a sound
of reconciliation coming directly from the throne. His previous book, *Prevail*, laid the foundation; *The More Excellent
Ministry* begins to build the house. (8 tapes available)

PRINCIPLES OF PRESENT TRUTH FROM GENESIS
— 76 pages (4 tapes). What is the Garden of Eden? What
is the spiritual significance of Noah's Ark? What are the
seven separations of Abraham? What is the Joseph Company? This book is a chapter-by-chapter analysis with an
emphasis upon Gen. 1-2 and the life of Abraham. It is the
seed-plot of the whole Bible.

PRINCIPLES OF PRESENT TRUTH FROM EXODUS-DEUTERONOMY — 152 pages (4 tapes). What are the three dimensions of the Passover principle? What are five ways to teach the Tabernacle of Moses? What is the significance of the seven Feasts of the Lord? What is the typology of the five major Offerings? Why should every pastor know about the garments of the High Priest? This book places major emphasis upon the Tabernacle of Moses, the Feasts, the Offerings, and the Priesthood. Many diagrams and charts facilitate these studies. Every Bible teacher has to be versed in this.

PRINCIPLES OF PRESENT TRUTH FROM JOSHUA-RUTH — 130 pages (4 tapes). What are principles for possessing the land? What is the Passover of Conquest? What is the significance of the fall of Jericho? Why are the Judges the forerunners of the Kingdom? How can we see in the Book of Ruth a detailed picture of the believer's walk from conception to perfection? This book contains a chapter-by-chapter analysis of Joshua and Judges, and a verse-by-verse study from the Book of Ruth. The entire text of Ruth, using the Hebrew text and other translations, is included. Many charts and diagrams.

PRINCIPLES OF PRESENT TRUTH FROM I-II SAMUEL, I CHRONICLES — 120 pages (4 tapes). Why is there an existing Eli and a growing Samuel? What is the typology of Saul as the old order and David as the new order? What is the panoramic significance of the story of David and Goliath? Why was Jonathan a picture of the man on the fence? What is the Tabernacle of David? This volume highlights Kingdom typology from these O.T. books, emphasizing the lives and the ministries of Samuel, Saul, David and Jonathan. Many charts and diagrams.

PRINCIPLES OF PRESENT TRUTH FROM I-II KINGS, II CHRONICLES — 130 pages (4 tapes). What is the typology of Solomon and his Temple? What is the Elijah ministry? What is the significance of the Sons of the Prophets? This book begins with an in-depth look at Solomon's reign with an emphasis upon the Temple. Each of the subsequent kings of Judah and Israel are analyzed, with an emphasis upon the ministry of the prophets, especially Elijah and Elisha.

PRINCIPLES OF PRESENT TRUTH FROM EZRA-ESTHER — 130 pages (4 tapes). How do these books of restoration parallel the restoration of the Church? What are the twelve gates of Nehemiah? Why does the rebuilding of walls picture the building of the human personality and the transformation of the soul? What is the typology of the Book of Esther and what does it have to do with the day of the Lord? Many charts and diagrams.

PRINCIPLES OF PRESENT TRUTH FROM JOB —118 pages (4 tapes). Pastor Varner considers this volume the most difficult work he has attempted. Why do the righteous suffer? Was God or the devil to blame for Job's plight? Why are Eliphaz, Bildad, and Zophar a picture of the soul of man? Why is Elihu a second-day ministry? Who are Behemoth and Leviathan? Why is Jesus our Heavenly Job? What is the significance of the restoration of Job? This book is a chapter-by-chapter and verse-by-verse study and is a most unique presentation.

PRINCIPLES OF PRESENT TRUTH FROM PSALMS 1-72 — 154 pages (4 tapes). Who wrote the psalms and how are they categorized? What kinds of musical instruments were used in the Bible? What is the importance of Zion and the Tabernacle of David? This book is a chapter-by-chapter and verse-by-verse study of each of these psalms. Outlines and background material is included with each chapter. A must for minstrels.

PRINCIPLES OF PRESENT TRUTH FROM PSALMS 73-150 — 156 pages (4 tapes). Who was Asaph? What is the significance of Psalm 119? What are the Songs of Degrees and how do they picture the believer's ascent into Zion or the ascent of the soul into union with the spirit? This book is a chapter-by-chapter and a verse-by-verse study of each of the remaining Psalms. A must for minstrels.

PRINCIPLES OF PRESENT TRUTH FROM PROVERBS — 118 pages (4 tapes). Why is Proverbs a book about sonship? How can we release the wisdom of God? What is the significance of the Strange Woman and the Virtuous Woman and how do these picture two kinds of minds? This volume includes a thorough introduction and a verse-by-verse study of chapters 1-9 and 30-31. It is great for young people, for chapters 10-29 are presented under 40 topical headings, analyzing areas of practical, daily Christian living.

PRINCIPLES OF PRESENT TRUTH FROM ECCLESIASTES AND THE SONG OF SOLOMON — 142 pages. Why is Ecclesiastes the book of the natural mind? Who is the Preacher? What is life under the sun? How is Ecclesiastes 12 a picture of an order or age that is dying? Who is the Shulamite? What is the relationship between Brideship and Sonship? How is the Song a picture of the development of the believer from conception to perfection? What are seven ways to teach the Song of Solomon? This book gives a thorough introduction to each of these neglected O.T. books. Many fresh insights are opened from Ecclesiastes. The Song is done verse-by-verse! It includes the entire text, other translations, key principles and a continuous story line! (4 tapes on Ecclesiates and 4 tapes on the Song of Solomon)

PRINCIPLES OF PRESENT TRUTH FROM ISAIAH 1-39 — 148 pages (4 tapes). Who was the man Isaiah? What is the Day of the Lord? Who is the Branch? What are the Seven Spirits of God? Who is Lucifer? What is the significance of Zion? This book furnishes a thorough introduction to the whole book of Isaiah. It is presented in a chapter-by-chapter, verse-by-verse format. An overview of all the prophetical books is included.

PRINCIPLES OF PRESENT TRUTH FROM ISAIAH 40-66 — 120 pages (4 tapes). Who is the Servant of Jehovah? Why does the Servant become servants after chapter 53? Who was Cyrus and what is the significant typology pertaining to him? How are Isaiah 58-66 an overview of the Feast of Tabernacles? What is the nation born in a day? This book furnishes a chapter-by-chapter and verse-by-verse study of the remaining chapters of Isaiah. A separate 20-tape series on a verse-by-verse study of Isaiah 53 also.

PRINCIPLES OF PRESENT TRUTH FROM JEREMIAH — 156 pages (8 tapes). Who was the man Jeremiah? How is he a prophet to the nations? How does this important book supplement the history of Kings and Chronicles? Who is the modern-day "Judah" to whom this message is sent? What is the significance of the potter's wheel? What about false pastors and shepherds? What is the meaning of each message to the various nations? What about the fall of Babylon? This book furnishes a chapter-by-chapter and verse-by-verse study of this important prophecy.

PRINCIPLES OF PRESENT TRUTH FROM EZEKIEL — 138 pages (8 tapes). This volume was co-authored with Bill Britton's notes. Why is Ezekiel an end-time book? What did Ezekiel see in chapter one? What is the glory of the Lord? What is the eschatological significance of chapters eight and nine? What are the cherubim? How do Ezekiel's prophecies to the nations compare with those of

Isaiah and Jeremiah? How does the prophet deal with false ministries in chapter 34? What about the New Covenant of chapter 36? What is the meaning of the vision of the dry bones? Who are Gog and Magog? What temple did Ezekiel see in chapters 40-48? How does this book compare to the Book of Revelation? This volume is a chapter-by-chapter and verse-by-verse treatment of the entire text of this neglected prophecy.

THE TABERNACLE OF MOSES — 100 pages (8 or 24 tapes). What are five ways to teach this pattern of heavenly things? Whose mansion is it? What is the significance of the Ark of the Covenant and the Most Holy Place? This book is filled with notes and outlines. This revelation must be mastered to fully understand the Word of God. Many drawings, charts, and outlines. A must for Bible teachers.

THE SERMON ON THE MOUNT — 50 pages (from 8 to 40 tapes). What is the Kingdom of God? How many kingdoms are there? What is the motive and the purpose of the Kingdom? Why is the Church the instrument of the Kingdom? This is an in-depth study of the Kingdom of God. It is a verse-by-verse study of Matthew 5-7, emphasizing the Beatitudes (the Preamble) and the principles (laws) of Christian living. This material will help a new believer and also challenge the more serious Bible student. Very practical. For those who want to know the purpose of the baptism of the Holy Ghost.

THE TONGUE OF THE LEARNED — with J. L. Dutton — over 60 pages (56 tapes to date). What is the preeminence of the Lord Jesus Christ? What does the Bible say about the Kingdom of God? How do we walk with the Lord? What does Scripture say about the Father-son relationship? What about the ministry of the Holy Spirit? Are the gifts of the Holy Spirit (a study of spiritual ministry) for us today? What are the Bible principles governing prayer, praise, and worship? What is the importance of the Church? What is the role and purpose of the Local Church? This book gives the definitions of 335 Bible terms under nine practical headings. It teaches the vocabulary of the Kingdom studied from the original languages of the Bible. Excellent for the classroom. Used in many Bible schools and churches, both here and abroad. If you have just been introduced to the Kingdom message, this volume is what you need.

CHOOSE YE THIS DAY: THE CONFLICTS OF JONATHAN — 34 pages (8 tapes). Why is Saul a picture of the old order? Why is Jonathan a hypocrite? What is the significance of the battle between David and Goliath? Is the Church the Seed of David? What does Saul's encounter with the witch of Endor have to do with the rise of the occult today? This book is in sermon form and tells of the life and ministry of the son of King Saul. A study of the old order and the new order from I Samuel 13-31. For the man on the fence.

THE HOLY GHOST BAPTISM — 35 pages (16 tapes). Who is the Holy Spirit? What is His ministry in the Old and New Testaments? Is the Holy Ghost Baptism a present reality for the Church? What are three New Testament purposes for speaking with tongues? How to minister and receive this experience. Excuses are answered with Scriptures. More answers are given to the most frequently asked questions. Bible terminology. Every pastor needs this book.

THE LAND AND THE THRONE — 44 pages (4 tapes). What is the significance of Jesus' being the Seed of Abraham and the Seed of David? What is the inheritance of the believer? Is it a mansion of gold or the multitude of the nations? This book is an in-depth study of the Abrahamic and Davidic Covenants. Jesus has the land and Jesus has the Throne. The Land is the Earth, and the Throne is the right to rule it! A return to Covenant Theology. Keys to eschatology.

THE HOUR IS COME — 28 pages (4 tapes). What is the glorification of the Son of man? Who is the corn of wheat? Why do we want to go to hell? How low will you go? This book in sermon form is an exegesis of John 12:20-33. A real challenge to world evangelism. The time is now!

THE TWELVE GATES OF THE CITY — 27 pages (16 tapes). Is the city of Revelation 21 a literal city? What is the Bible truth about Heaven? What about the mansions and the golden streets? The gates of pearl? How does the Christ nature progressively unfold from within the believer? How does the city come from heaven to earth, from the invisible to the visible realm? This book of notes is a verse-by-verse study of Revelation 21. The old order concept of Heaven is examined. The city is a people. A study of Genesis 49 and the sons of Jacob — from Reuben to Benjamin. For teachers.

THE POWER OF THE FLAMING SWORD — 21 pages (8 tapes). What is the flaming sword? How powerful are the words which we speak? What does the Bible have to say about the sword? This book in sermon form is a message concerning our speaking the creative Word of the Lord. This is emphasized in the areas of prayer, praise, and prophecy.

THE IMPORTANCE OF THE HOME AND FAMILY— 30 pages (1 tape). What is the importance of the home as the basic unit of society? What is the parallel between the home and the Local Church? What are the two institutions that God has ordained and what is the order of authority in each? What is the significance of the home being a wineskin? What connection is there between the Elijah ministry and the home? This book in sermon form is the first of 12.

A LAMB FOR A HOUSE — 39 pages (1 tape). What is God's method of bringing a nation out of bondage? What

is the Passover of the Kingdom? What are the characteristics of the lamb? What about spiritual immunity?
This book in sermon form is an exegesis of Exodus 12
and is an excellent study about the home and family.
Good for pastors and teachers.

KINGDOM PRINCIPLES FOR THE HOME — 43
pages (1 tape). What is the principle of love? What is the
principle of mutual respect? What is the principle of
open communication? This book in sermon form gives a
unique study of the Bible definition of love from the New
Testament Greek of I Corinthians 13:1-13 (plus the use of
several other translations).

SKYWALKERS — 44 pages (8 tapes). What examples for
teenagers are provided in Samuel, David, Esther, Ruth,
Joash, Jesus and others? How can our young people live
in the heavenlies today? This study was prepared by Pastor Varner for our teens. He was assisted by Sue Baird.
Other local churches are now using this series to teach
their young people. This very practical class was taught
as part of the curriculum of our Christian school.

DARE TO BE DIFFERENT — 30 pages (8 tapes).
Another good book for teens, this was presented in our
Christian school. There are two kingdoms. We must
dare to be different in our attitude, obedience, joy,
meditation, dependability, gratefulness, discernment,
perception, enthusiasm, kindness, forgiveness, modes-
ty and boldness. These are characteristics of young
people who are walking in the Kingdom of God. These
13 lessons are also excellent Sunday school material.

FOUR FOUNDATIONS OF EFFECTUAL PRAYER—
24 pages (8 tapes). There is a tremendous emphasis on
prayer at this time. Here is examined a familiar subject
from a fresh perspective. We need to understand prayer
from God's side of the Covenant. His thanksgiving for
us, His righteousness to us, His boldness through us, and

His compassion among us are four principles which must be understood.

A VISION OF YOUR WORTH — 28 pages (4 tapes). Every Christian must know His worth in Christ. Worthy is the Lamb! What is the worthy portion? What does it mean to be counted worthy? Who is the lambkin? The answers to these questions will help the believer to become all he can in the Lord.

SING, O BARREN — 28 pages (4 tapes). God wants every one of us to be fruitful. We can see keys to this by studying the lives of Sarah, Rebekah, Rachel, Manoah's wife, Hannah, Elizabeth and Mary. We must travail so that the Christ within us can be formed. There are seven powerful truths coming forth from the Body of Christ.

THE RAPTURE — 40 pages (12 tapes). An up-to-date look at Daniel's prophecy of Seventy Weeks and a fresh re-examination of contemporary eschatology.

PRAISE TABERNACLE
CORRESPONDENCE COURSE

UNDERSTANDING THE KING AND HIS KINGDOM — A one-, two-, or three-year study program — "36 Steps Toward Your Understanding the Bible." Certificates will be given for the completion of each of the first two years and a diploma for the completion of the third year. Write today for your free brochure.

Additional Available Tape Series

Jesus, Lord of the Home (12 tapes)
Are You Ready for the Third Dimension? (8 tapes)
Israel: God's Chosen People (8 tapes)
The Kingdom of God (8 tapes)
Spiritual Ministry (12 tapes)
Servant Power (8 tapes)
Four-fold Definition of the Local Church (16 tapes)

The New Testament Local Church (32 tapes)
Halloween, Christmas, Easter (8 tapes)
God's Two Greatest Mysteries (8 tapes)
The Coming of the Lord (12 tapes)
Women's Ministry (8 tapes)
The Book of Acts (8 tapes)
Principles of Kingdom Finance (8 tapes)
Bible Patterns of the Kingdom (12 tapes)
The Faith of God (8 tapes)
The Five-fold Ministry (12 tapes)
Life and Immortality (12 tapes)
Water Baptism (8 tapes)
The Day of Atonement (8 tapes)
Principles of Restoration (12 tapes)
The Will of God (8 tapes)
The Songs of Degrees (16 tapes)
The Emerging Christ (12 tapes)
Apostolic Principles (12 tapes)
Romans, Verse-by-verse (from 8 to 30 tapes)
The Feast of Tabernacles (16 tapes)
The More Excellent Ministry (8 tapes) — these are the
    original tapes preached at the House of Prayer in 1981

TAPE OF THE MONTH

Each month two cassette tapes are made available by
Pastor Varner. These messages are ministered by him
and others in the five-fold ministry. You may join this
growing list of listeners on a monthly offering basis.

VIDEO CASSETTES

We are just beginning this new avenue of ministry.
Presently available are three two-hour video cassettes on

the Book of Ruth. This teaching is a verse-by-verse exegesis concerning the Christian walk from conception to perfection, from birth to maturity. Please write or call for more information.

SEMINARS AND CONVENTIONS

There are annual meetings here in Richlands for the Body of Christ. Please inquire for information on the next meeting. There is a team of ministry here at Praise Tabernacle that is available to your local church to teach the principles of restoration and assist in the areas of praise and worship. Please contact Pastor Varner.